EBURY PRESS

FABULOUS FEASTS, FABLES AND FAMILY

Tabinda Jalil Burney is a writer, translator and doctor, working in the National Health Service in the UK. She is the author of *How to Feed your Child (and Enjoy it!)*, also published in Hindi, which won the Gourmand World Cookbooks Award 2012 for Best Children and Family Cookbook. She has also translated numerous Urdu short stories into English as part of various published anthologies. Her keen interest in Urdu poetry, her nostalgia for her family's food and culture and a desire to delve into the family's history have inspired her to write this book.

Celebrating 35 Years of
Penguin Random House India

'This book is a precious insight into a household and its unique cuisine; the food reminds me of my own childhood. Beautifully written, the recipes are of family favourites—dishes packed with layers and stories'—Asma Khan

'Tabinda works at her magic loom, weaving a gossamer-like fabric that catches glints of light from different angles and shimmers, casting a mesmerizing spell. This memoir reminds us that food alone doesn't make a feast. It's the shared excitement, effort and laughter in the family that memories are made of. Luminous words resonate with echoes of forgotten folk songs and nonsense lyrics as the author takes a zig-zag, slow and scenic route to mouthwatering recipes. Digressions on hand-hemmed costumes are mini dissertations—rare sparkling gems. A fabulous feast—this book of many delights'—Pushpesh Pant

'This is a captivating book that takes readers on an enchanting journey through a world filled with magical feasts, ancient fables and extraordinary characters'—Rocky Mohan

'In my mind I have visited this home, a rambling old house in Aligarh at least half a dozen times, sometimes listening to family gossip over a handful of intensely sour kakronda berries in the courtyard. At other times, huddled beneath a velvet quilt with a profusion of cousins, listening to ghost stories after a two-hour dinner, during which kebabs, saalans and qormas disappeared in no time at all. That is the immediacy of Tabinda's fascinating narrative'—Marryam H. Reshii

fabulous feasts, fables and family

a culinary memoir

TABINDA JALIL BURNEY

EBURY
PRESS

An imprint of Penguin Random House

EBURY PRESS

USA | Canada | UK | Ireland | Australia
New Zealand | India | South Africa | China | Singapore

Ebury Press is part of the Penguin Random House group of companies
whose addresses can be found at global.penguinrandomhouse.com

Published by Penguin Random House India Pvt. Ltd
4th Floor, Capital Tower 1, MG Road,
Gurugram 122 002, Haryana, India

Penguin
Random House
India

First published in Ebury Press by Penguin Random House India 2023

Copyright © Tabinda Jalil Burney 2023

ISBN 9780143462316

Typeset in Goudy Old Style by Manipal Technologies Limited, Manipal
Printed at Gopsons Papers Pvt. Ltd., Noida

www.penguin.co.in

MIX
Paper from
responsible sources
FSC® C191020

Contents

Family Tree   vii

Glossary   ix

Introduction   xv

Nashta   1

Amma's Kakronda Qeema   12

Nasho Khala's Velvety Kofte   25

Abba's Favourite Kali Gajar ka Halwa   43

Mummy's Special Shami Kebab   59

Naseem Khala's Extraordinary Firni   76

Ruqqaiyya Khala's Gratifying Chuqandar Gosht   92

Azeemuddin's Istoo   106

Shahida Chachi's Spectacular Rasawal   119

Najma Khala's Splendid Kaleji   135

Rana Momani's Suji Halwa Squares   150

Nanno's Maash ki Dal   165

STORIES

Bandariya Bahuriya	181
The Tale of Haji Baghlol	187
The Fable of Mama Qamas	193
The Legend of Noble Naseem and Cunning Husnara	196
Raja Bakarkana, the Goat-Eared King	200
The Tale of Sharif Khan and Badmash Khan	203
The Lioness and the Ewe	207
The Ghost Who Lisped	210
Acknowledgements	213

Family Tree

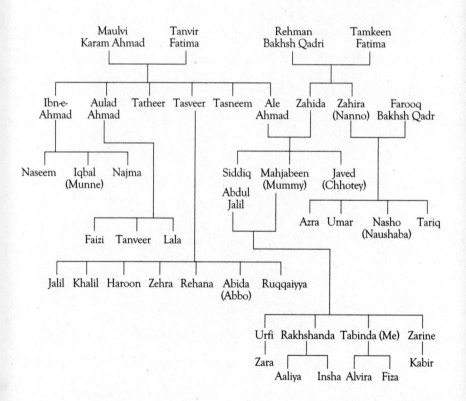

Glossary

aangan:	Courtyard, an open space within the home
ahmaqon:	Idiots
Amma:	Literally, mother. We called our maternal grandmother, Amma
asli ghee:	Pure clarified butter
athlas:	An expensive, glossy fabric
baqi:	Remaining
bargad:	Banyan tree
bari:	Little packets or pouches filled with sweets, nuts and chhuarey that a groom's family distributes to guests at the time of a wedding
batua:	A purse made of fabric, usually with a drawstring feature
beshqeemti:	Priceless
chaadar:	A sheet of cloth, also worn as a draped head covering.
Chhilka:	The outer covering
chhuarey:	Dried dates
chingari:	A spark

choolha:	A floor-level cooking device, made out of mud in the olden days, but it could also refer to a stove or hob now. The mud version used wood as fuel and the cooking pot was placed on top, straddling the edges.
chowki:	A low, square divan, used mostly for sitting during the day time
dastarkhwan:	A large, square or rectangular piece of cloth around which people would eat their meal, sitting on the floor, the cloth would sometimes be printed with verses
gajra:	Fragrant flowers threaded together on a string, used as a decorative hair accessory by women
ghaas phhoos:	Hay/dried grass
ghorhi:	A mare or female pony
gobhi:	Cauliflower or cabbage
goley:	Balls or rounds of any material
haath baande:	With folded holds, in subservience
hamd:	praise to Allah
hisaab:	Arithmetic, calculation
iman:	Faith
imli:	Tamarind
itr:	Perfume
jhoomar:	a piece of jewellery worn on the forehead; *teeka*
kachori:	A deep-fried savoury snack with a spicy filling
kakronda:	A sour berry, akin to cranberries
kaliyan:	Buds of flowers, also panels of fabric for an outfit, to be sewn together
kamkhwab:	Brocade, made with silk

kangoorey:	(plural) a domed or curved edge of an item of clothing, fabric or even a building. Singular, kangoora
kebabi:	One who makes seekh kebabs on skewers
keechad bhari nali:	A drain full of mud
keorah:	A cooking ingredient; fragrant extract of screwpine flowers
khaat:	A woven cot or charpoy
khichda:	A sumptuous dish made with pounded wheat, lentils, richly spiced and served with a delectable bhuna gosht, caramelized onions, a twist of lime, chopped green chillies and a dollop of yoghurt
khwab:	Dream
laadli:	A much indulged and fawned upon girl
lacchey:	Loops or layers
langar:	A free meal served to travelling masses
mainyyon:	Also known as *manjha*; a muslim pre-wedding ritual
marmareen:	Like marble
martban:	A large, glazed pottery jar, used for pickling or storing food or water, usually with a lid
masjid:	A mosque
mithai:	A generic term for Indian sweetmeats
momani:	The wife of one's mother's brother
muhavrey:	Sayings or proverbs, usually colloquial and region-specific
murgh mutanjan:	Murgh refers to chicken and mutanjan is an unusual, sweet chicken and rice dish. In this context it refers to an elaborate feast with a complicated preparation.

naayab:	Unparalleled, rare
nakhh:	A resin, gently smouldered to release a perfumed smoke
namakpara:	A fried, salty snack made with flour
nargisi koftey:	A coating of minced meat around a hard-boiled egg, served as a curry
nazar:	Vision or sight. Also refers to the evil eye
nazariye:	Outlooks
neematkhana:	A wooden cupboard used to store food; a larder
nek:	Honest
pankha:	A hand-held fan. It can also refer to an electric fan attached to the ceiling
petha:	A sweetmeat made with gourd, a kind of pumpkin; a speciality of the city of Agra
phhool bootey:	Flowers and tender shoots
phulkiyan:	Deep-fried balls of spicy chickpea flour batter
qalai:	A process of coating brass and copper utensils with tin using chemicals and heat, imparting a bright sheen to the surface
qandeel:	A colourful paper lantern, lit with candle or oil lamp inside
qasai:	A butcher
qatli:	A slice or well-defined piece of an edible substance
rani haar:	An eleborate necklace
razai:	A light quilt, filled with cotton wool
rishta:	A proposal of marriage and also means a relationship
rumal:	Handkerchief

rumali roti:	A very thin and large Indian bread, served with curries
saalan:	A generic word for a meat-based curry, the main dish of a meal. It could be vegetable based too.
sabziwallah:	Vegetable-seller
salwar-qameez:	A women's outfit comprising of gathered trousers and a tunic
seo:	Also known as sev; delicate, deep fried strands of spicy chickpea flour batter.
seth:	A wealthy merchant
shakarpara:	A sweet deep-fried snack made with sugar and flour
sher:	A couplet, form of poetry
shifaa:	Healing, medical treatment
sunaar:	A goldsmith who makes and sells gold jewellery
sutli:	Twine or jute rope
taaq:	A recess or niche in a wall, used to place objects
tabalchi:	One who plays the tabla
tabla:	Indian drums, played by hand, set in pairs. Similar to bongos
tarkeeb:	Trick or method
tashtari:	A platter
taubah:	An exclamation of repenting and vowing to sin no more
than:	A bolt or roll of fabric, bought wholesale and cut as required
thumri:	A genre of Indian classical music

tola and masha: Old weight measurements, especially referring to gold jewellery

zarda: A celebratory sweet dish made with rice, sugar and nuts, dyed a bright saffron

Introduction

Growing up, we had spells of idyllic times during the school holidays, spent at the sprawling home of our maternal grandparents in Aligarh, Uttar Pradesh. For us city dwellers, bound by the routines of school and studies, it was a very welcome respite. Looking back, those times have influenced us in countless ways. There was a massive collection of books in my grandfather's personal library—some dusty and worn, others pristine, both in English and Urdu. We also came into contact with scholars, writers and poets who came to visit our grandparents. Over the years, we came to respect these talented people for their wit, knowledge and wisdom, but we also observed their quirks that made them seem human and familiar. There was always a steady stream of visitors, including some members of the extended family who lived locally and whose lives and the minutiae of their existence were of great importance to my grandmother, whom we called Amma. Some of these relatives had children who were our age, and we played the childhood games that children from our generation played—before the advent of mobile phones and electronic devices. We hardly ever watched television and as for the grown-ups, there were always spirited discussions about books, writers, poets, and yes, sometimes good old gossip too! Another popular post-dinner entertainment was *bait bazi*, a game involving people reciting couplets or shers in a chain, with each successive player reciting a sher that begins with the last letter of the sher recited by the previous player. There was much mirth as a player got stuck with a 'difficult' letter and tried to squirm out of it by using an improvised or fabricated sher! Our grandfather, Abba, who was himself a much-celebrated poet, knew thousands of shers, and it was fascinating to hear him recite the appropriate one effortlessly, in his characteristically impressive and sonorous voice.

This household could by no means be called a traditional Muslim household, but there were many habits and customs that we, as a family, adapted to our lives, over the generations. These make their presence felt in many aspects of our lives today, even though we are now spread across the globe and have married outside the main family tree into various other cultures and backgrounds. Our provenance asserts itself from time to time in the food we eat and relish, the figures of speech we unthinkingly use, the jewellery and clothing we prefer at family celebrations, the bedtime stories we tell our children and in countless other aspects of our lives. Even though it may be diluted now by living abroad, or outside of UP, in bigger cities, we still have the invisible yet very strong bonds that link us to our childhood.

Food is inextricably linked to nostalgia. The sights, smells, tastes or even the mere mention of a particular food can sometimes trigger vivid memories. The joys of plucking and biting into a ripe guava from a tree in the courtyard, the magically savoury aroma emanating from a platter of freshly made shami kebabs, with the slightly pungent notes of sliced raw onions on top, the intensely earthy flavour and vivid, deep magenta colour of chuqandar gosht, the almost decadent, rich flavour of the biryani at a family wedding, followed by some seriously indulgent melt-in-the-mouth gulatthi dessert in fragrant earthenware bowls, the crisp, almost fragile caramelized and browned onions, fried in ghee, perched daintily over a piping hot, fluffy mound of moong ki dal khichdi, alongside a spoonful of fiery, vibrant coriander chutney.

Many of these dishes were made at home and were part of the everyday fare, along with hot rotis. Some, like the sheermal, a soft and slightly sweet bread, were bought from a local bakery to accompany a sumptuous home-made qorma and sometimes seekh kebabs were bought from a local kebabi, who made these delicate, finger-shaped kebabs on hot skewers over burning coals, fanning the embers with a well-worn hand-held, woven bamboo *pankha*. These were quickly wrapped in old newspapers and handed over to be enjoyed at home, piping hot. Sometimes, there would be a stack of rumali rotis too, the name of which caused much mirth, and they were nicknamed 'hankie rotis' by the more puerile of us. The strong and pungent smells from the kebabs were fascinating and exciting, as if a drama were about to unfold. There would be thin rings of raw onion sent along with the kebabs, which further added to the aroma.

Some of the dishes were made by extremely talented home cooks, ladies from our extended family, who cooked a special dish to bring over, especially if their proficiency in making that dish was well known in the family circle, and who then rejoiced in the compliments that would invariably follow. Each such triumph would further seal their status of completely 'owning' that dish, so much so that, over the years, one came to associate a particular dish with that aunt or grand-aunt who would always make it. The recipes for these would have been closely guarded and passed down through the generations, but no one used a recipe book or even measured out quantities. They cooked with what they had at home, what was in season, and used a rough guide to feed the number of people that the dish was meant for. Even though there was a dining table with straight-backed wooden chairs, it was usually just used for breakfast or if fewer people were there for lunch. Most times, when we had extended family over (there was usually a sizeable number of people, including us), we would sit cross-legged on a large, fairly low wooden *chowki*, covered with *chandni*, a plain white sheet, and tuck into the spread in front of us. Sometimes there would be a *dastarkhwan*, or tablecloth, spread over the chowki. Amma had an enviably massive collection of porcelain dinner sets, with ornamental plates in various designs that, over the years, had lost a few brethren. So we ate on beautiful, often mismatched, antique crockery, using our hands, amid great laughter and conviviality. For *meetha*, or dessert, if there was any room left after that sumptuous meal, it was invariably the famous Aligarh gazak from the local Taj sweets—a delicate flaky flattened creation made with sesame seeds and sold in cardboard boxes. Sometimes, there would be a home-made halwa, either suji, gajar or lauki, and in season, much to Abba's delight, *kali* (black) gajar.

The chowki occupied a large space in the covered veranda (that had a fine *jaali*, or net, on the latticed wrought iron grille to keep the flies and mosquitoes out), which looked out into a courtyard where there were a few fruit trees. There was a tamarind tree, a guava tree and a large thorny bush with very sour berries called kakronda, which draped itself lustily along the kitchen wall and reached the roof. As children, we would eat these berries, putting a few in our pockets and giggling as we watched each other wrinkle our faces when biting into the berries and experiencing their sudden, sharp sourness. Amma being a naturally creative person, cooked these berries with lamb mince—called simply qeema kakronda—which was a brilliant creation as the sourness not only became more pleasant and less intense, it also cut through the unctuousness of the mince and balanced everything. I have never had this combination elsewhere, as at our own home in Delhi, it was more usual to pair the qeema with peas, potatoes or fenugreek leaves.

Of course, no day would be complete without snuggling up with Amma on her large, heavy wooden bed with a carved headboard, comprising a series of polished, upright, smooth spindles, through which we would love to entangle our fingers. There was a plethora of pillows in various sizes, each with dainty hand-embroidered motifs and a hand-crocheted edging. Spread over it was a thin *razai* (quilt) in the summer months, with a delicate, slender layer of puffy cotton wool and usually made from old, well-worn saris, which had loose running stitch work with a white cotton thread in oblique lines through it, called *tagai*. The border, which was roughly the width of an outstretched palm, was usually made with a contrasting colour of fabric called *got* (pronounced as goat). Again, Amma's thrifty ways, as was the norm for everyone in those days, came into play, and many of the clothes that even the smallest of us had outgrown or inadvertently ripped were recycled. For instance, a nice shiny salwar qameez from a few Eids ago had now become *utanga* (one of the many words I had only ever heard Amma use, but which we freely use now). Utanga refers to an item of clothing that has become too small in length for the wearer. The stitched outfit would be painstakingly unravelled and cut into wide strips, which would then be joined together with obliquely running seams, called *jorh*.

It was always comforting to see a much-loved but unusable item get a new lease on life, and we also loved to spot our frocks or shirts in a patchwork quilt or *razai*. In the winter months, there were heavier *lihaafs* with a thicker padding of cotton wool that were periodically sent over to a *dhunna* to fluff out the cotton and get rid of flat or lumpy bits. Using a freshly fluffed lihaaf was like encasing yourself in the softest, warmest, comfiest cocoon imaginable, akin to drifting away on a cloud.

Whatever the season, Amma's bed was the place to be if you wanted to listen to her stories or *qissas*. The thing about Amma's stories was that they were never sickly-sweet tales, nor were they moralistic or even religious. They had a Roald Dahl-esque quality to them, in the sense that they were not always conventionally suitable for children; they could be dark and subversive, with a sprinkling of bloodshed and gore, and the characters didn't always live happily ever after in castles. The stories could be set in a forest, a poor man's hut or even a busy street in a town. There were astonishing stories of djinns that were scary and fascinating in equal measure. I am not sure if these stories were completely original or were previously read by her in a magazine and retold, but for me and all my siblings, they will forever remain Amma's stories.

Nashta

It is a bright, sunny morning at Amma's house. There is general clatter from the kitchen. I have been woken and am heading towards the dining room. There are numerous bookshelves and glass-fronted wooden cabinets along the corridor, all crammed with books. I reach the dining room. There are framed pictures of our grandparents' family and friends. Mamu is a keen amateur photographer and has painstakingly captured our childhood moments and displayed them on walls, tables and shelves. Most of them are black and white photographs, some just of one person, seemingly caught unawares and not at their best, while others are posed group pictures of people stiffly standing or sitting and smiling at the camera. The frames are simple wooden ones or silvery metal ones in various sizes.

Our usual breakfast in Aligarh is mattree, or Aligarh wale biscuit, as they are popularly known to all. They are less of a biscuit and more of a rusk. Circular and fairly large, the size of an adult palm, they are crisp and yet spongy within, slightly sweet and a beautiful golden brown in colour, like toast. There is a subtle hint of cardamom and fennel seeds that is enticing and unique. They are baked and sold in rolled-up paper wrappers with a coloured paper label stuck on top of the packet. To rip open a fresh packet of mattree, slather on lashings of salty butter and eat them is absolute heaven! They are sensational simply with butter but they can also be eaten with a generous spread of jam or with thinly sliced boiled eggs and a sprinkle of freshly ground pepper. A packet can easily feed a large family and have a couple left over for the next day, though they do tend to go a bit limp by then. We usually have them with steaming mugs of tea and a few sliced guavas. The famous 'Diggi ke amrood' are a class apart. Larger than average, with firm flesh and a vibrant green, somewhat knobbly skin, these are the best guavas I have ever tasted. We make it a point to buy a large bag of these whenever we head back to Delhi, along with some gazak, of course, to remind us of the glorious times.

Various newspapers in Urdu and English lie neatly folded for Abba, along with his morning cup of tea, near his favourite chair, next to the chowki. It is a curious-looking chair, and I love to sit in it when it is unoccupied. It is a solid wood recliner with an angled backrest, and each of the armrests has a further hinged limb, which tucks neatly under the armrest when not in use but can be splayed out and used as a table to perch a book or a cup of tea on. It has a cane rattan weave on the seat and back and is covered with enormous cushions that fit the chair, so it is the most comfortable pod to sink into when one is reading or, in my case, daydreaming.

We are all home today. It is a lazy Sunday morning, and the day ahead stretches languidly without purpose or plan. There are intense discussions between Amma and Sakina, the cook, about what will be cooked for lunch. A *sabziwallah* calls out at the gates, and Sakina hurries to buy some fresh vegetables from him to cook that day. She will go to the local *qasai* (butcher) later to get some gosht (meat). She is a tall, robust lady who wears a loose salwar qameez and has a chaadar draped over her head.

A metal nose ring adorns her sombre face, and she speaks in a rural dialect of Urdu. She addresses Amma as 'Begum Saab'.

Today, we are having roghani tikiyan for breakfast, along with alu ke warq.

Roghani tikiyan are flatbreads cooked on a griddle. They are smaller than average rotis and not as greasy and heavy as puris. They have a beautiful reddish-brown colour, and the dough is enriched with ghee or oil while kneading to make it soft. The tikiyan are rolled out into small rounds and carefully pricked with the prongs of a fork so that, unlike a phulka or roti, they do not fluff up. They keep well on long train journeys, and we often pack them along on picnics too. Shakoor Chacha calls them gulabi tikiyan and is a huge fan of them. He is a foodie and greatly relishes rich qormas and elaborate biryanis. A doctor by profession, he nevertheless gorges on rich niharis, kebabs and similar decadent and sumptuous foods on a regular basis.

Alu, or potatoes, are extremely versatile and ubiquitous, readily and adroitly partnering most vegetables and meats with excellent results. We are just as likely to savour alu gobhi or alu sem for our meal as we are to savour alu gosht. Boiled, fried or cooked in a gravy, potatoes lend themselves to myriad uses in Amma's kitchen. Boiled and mashed, they go in the spicy stuffing of samosas. Wrapped around a mound of cooked qeema, they make delicious cutlets. Cooked with boiled eggs when there is no fresh meat, they pair nicely with andey alu ka shorba, known these days as egg curry. To bulk up qeema, they pair up readily as chunks. Today we are having a very pared-down version of alu, a dish that is so comforting and satisfying that it belies its simplicity and ease of preparation. It is called alu ke warq. Of course, it is the simplest of things that provide boundless joy, and they are also the ones that are tough to get absolutely right!

Unlike the runny, gravy-based alu that we eat with hot, fluffy puris and have given the moniker 'station waley alu', these are devoid of the ubiquitous haldi or turmeric that is at the heart of any Indian dal or sabzi, imparting a vivid yellow colour to a dish. The spices are also minimal. And instead of red chilli powder or tomatoes, which lend a fiery red colour to a dish, these have the smoky, intense flavour of whole dried red chillies. Pale, but definitely very interesting. There is nothing pallid or bland about this dish, and the humble potato is deservingly the star of the show. The flavour is hearty, robust and intensely satisfying, and the discs of raw, peeled potato not only hold their shape but also acquire a faintly buttery, savoury and hearty character that simply must be experienced first-hand to fully believe it.

Roghani Tikiyan

The word roghani comes from the Urdu word roghan, which means buttery, grease-laden and rich. It can also be served with andey ka khageena (similar to scrambled eggs but spiked with green chillies, finely chopped tomatoes and coriander leaves) for breakfast. This is the way it was cooked in Amma's house, but some people also like to add a spoonful of leftover saalan, or gravy, from the night before to add flavour, richness and fragrance.

Makes about 6
300 gm atta
salt to taste
a pinch of ajwain, crushed between the palms
4 tbsp full cream milk, and ideally a dollop of balai (skimmed off cream left after boiling milk)
1 tsp *asli* (pure) ghee

For the topping:
a few strands of saffron, soaked in 1 tbsp warm milk
½ tsp sugar

Mix the atta, ajwain and salt in a bowl, and then add the ghee and balai, if using. Bring these together until the mixture resembles grainy crumbs. Gradually add the milk little by little and knead into a firm dough. Cover with a plate or cloth and let it rest for about 15 minutes.

Divide the dough into 6 small balls. Roll them out to a size that is bigger than a puri but smaller than a regular roti.

Use a fork to make several shallow indentations on each tikiyan. This prevents them from puffing up while being cooked.

Place the tikiyan on a medium-hot tawa and press down on both sides until cooked—a few brown spots should appear on the surface. No oil or ghee is used in the cooking.

For the final flourish, mix the saffron soaked in warm milk with sugar and dip a clean, bunched-up kitchen cloth in it.

Lightly dab each tiki on either side with this mixture for a gorgeous fragrance and flavour.

The tikiyan can be eaten hot off the pan by themselves or along with some alu ke warq. This makes a sumptuous and filling breakfast or brunch.

Alu ke Warq

3-4 medium-sized potatoes
1-2 whole dried red chillies
salt to taste
3-4 black peppercorns

½ tsp cumin seeds
1 tbsp cooking oil of your choice
fresh coriander leaves for garnish (optional)

Peel and thinly slice the potatoes into rounds and set aside in a bowl of cold water.

In a karahi, heat the oil and add the cumin seeds. Wait until they sizzle, and then throw in the whole dried red chillies.

Add the potatoes after draining out the water. Gently mix with a wooden spoon. Add salt and black peppercorns. Add about 100 ml of water.

Cook covered for about 10 minutes on low heat.

Very gently check to see if it's done. If required, cook for a few more minutes.

Check the seasoning and serve garnished with chopped coriander leaves.

As Abba is retired now and we are on our school holidays, breakfasts tend to be relaxed, unrushed and convivial. It is wonderful to be able to sit together and savour these wonderful and special occasions. The makhan ki goli, a salty and creamy variant of the regular butter we have back home, is another Aligarh speciality. We love to slather it over our mattree or toast.

As for jam, Amma is an expert jam maker, and there are always bottles of delicious home-made jams made with whatever fruit is abundant, cheap and readily available. Of course, we kids are recruited to wash, dice and stone the vast quantities of fruit. These are then poured into sterilized glass jars and sealed off. It is quite a fun game to try to discover what kind of fruit has been used in a bottle of jam. Amma airily dismisses it with 'mixed fruit', which means she threw in all kinds of fruit that she had on hand. Sometimes there would be orange marmalade, tart and glossy, with slivers of orange peel, or a deep ruby-coloured plum jam spiced with cloves that Amma assured us was very *mufeed* (beneficial, good for you). It was henceforth referred to as mufeed jam!

Apart from this 'heavenly breakfast', there are other *nashta* dishes that are often made in Amma's home.

Khageena

(*Our version of scrambled eggs*)

3 eggs
1 large onion, finely sliced
1 tomato, finely chopped
1–2 green chillies, finely chopped
½ tsp red chilli powder
salt to taste
freshly ground black peppercorns
2 tbsp oil
a bunch of fresh coriander leaves

Heat the oil in a large pan and add the onions. Sauté these for a few minutes until they turn translucent.

Meanwhile, crack the eggs into a bowl and add the spices, chillies and tomato.

Transfer the eggs to the pan and cook them gently, breaking them up and mixing them until they acquire a texture similar to scrambled eggs.

Once cooked, transfer to a dish and sprinkle with chopped fresh coriander leaves.

Kharboozey ki Kashtiyan

(Melon boats)

These are refreshing and light, greatly suited for a summer breakfast. Ripe, small melons with orange-coloured flesh work best, such as cantaloupes, ambrosias or honeydews. They are fragrant and naturally sweet and have softer flesh, making them ideal for this recipe. Many breakfast items tend to be seasonal. Light and refreshing in summer, and warming ones for winter.

4 melons
sugar to taste
crushed ice cubes
rose water

Wash the melons and halve them horizontally.

Scoop out the seeds and the fibrous material surrounding them.

Cup the halved melon in your palm, and with a fork, mash up the melon flesh right to the edges and the bottom.

Add sugar as desired and a drop of rose water.

Coarsely crush a few ice cubes and place them in the melon bowls.

In a few minutes, you will have a chilled and intensely refreshing treat.

Hari Matar ki Ghugni

In season, fresh green peas are painstakingly shelled in heaps and magically turned into this warming and nutritious dish. Served as a snack any time of the day, this also makes an excellent winter breakfast, on its own or with hot, flaky parathas.

2 cups shelled fresh peas
1 tbsp oil
½ tsp cumin seeds
1–2 green chillies, finely chopped
a small piece of ginger, finely grated
a few black peppercorns, coarsely ground
salt to taste
juice of half a lemon

Heat the oil in a karahi. Add the cumin seeds, and as they splutter, add the peas and a tablespoon or so of water.

Cover and cook for 6–8 minutes, until the peas are cooked and appear slightly wrinkled.

Add the salt, pepper, ginger and green chillies. Ginger aids digestion and also adds a subtle hum of fiery heat.

The green chillies help retain the dark green colour of the peas.

Once cooked, serve in individual small bowls with a squeeze of lemon.

Dal Bhari Roti or Birhain

Another great traditional UP breakfast item, this one is specially made during the monsoon season. Eaten on its own with a generous smear of home-made white butter or with an exquisite raw mango chutney, this is a wonderful accompaniment to the sounds of lashing rain and birdsong, paired with cups of steaming tea.

1 cup chana dal, soaked for a few hours
1 small onion, finely chopped
½ tsp dried mango powder
¾ tsp red chilli powder
½ tsp cumin powder
a small bunch of fresh coriander leaves, finely chopped
salt to taste
ghee (optional)

For the roti:
2 cups atta
salt to taste
water for kneading

Knead the roti dough as usual and keep it aside, covered.

Boil the dal along with red chilli powder, salt, cumin powder and a little water until it is cooked. It should be dry, not watery, and easily pressed between the fingers and thumb.

Transfer the dal to a bowl and mash it with a wooden spoon or masher. Once it is a smooth and thick paste, add the chopped onion, coriander leaves and dried mango powder. Mix everything together well and check the seasoning.

Portion the dough into roughly lemon-sized balls.

Flatten each ball and place a portion of the dal filling in the centre. Bring the edges together and carefully roll out each roti.

Cook the rotis on a tawa, adding a smidgen of asli ghee to each as they come off the griddle.

Best eaten hot with mango chutney (see below).

Ambiya ki Chutney

Ambiya, also known as kairi, is an unripe mango that is pale yellow in flesh and quite sour. It is also used in making pickles and lots of cooling summer drinks.

2 unripe mangoes
1 tbsp sugar or grated jaggery
1 tsp nigella seeds
½ tsp fennel seeds
½ tsp red chilli powder
salt to taste
1 tbsp vinegar

Wash, peel and stone the mango.

Cut the flesh into very small pieces. Alternatively, grate the chunks of flesh.

In a small pan, bring together all the above, stirring continuously on a low flame until it comes together as a sticky, dark chutney with a jam-like consistency.

Amma's Kakronda Qeema

Like many things that happen serendipitously, this too came into being because the opportunity presented itself. There is a large bush of these very sour, pinkish-white berries, known as kakronda, quite similar to cranberries, that spreads itself luxuriantly on the outer wall of the kitchen. The kitchen overlooks the courtyard. We often play there and grab a kakronda or two while dashing off to climb on the roof. There is a hand pump next to the bush, and the novelty of an open-air water source complete with a quirky, curved, wrought iron handle is still new and exciting for us city dwellers. There is a whooshing sound when you pull and then push the handle, and a jet of clean water comes gushing out from a wide-bore tap. There is a neat, grey raised square, a boundary made of cement, around the pump. Overripe berries fall around this hand pump like raindrops and often get squashed like insects underfoot by the various people who use it.

Qeema is made quite often in Amma's home. It is minced mutton and is used in making all sorts of kebabs or as a dish on its own in its naturally soft, granular form. Usually green peas, if in season, are added for a contrast and to make it more substantial, or potato chunks, fenugreek (methi) leaves or it is made as a dopiyaza, a runny qeema dish made with masses of onion. Qeema is a popular mealtime staple, easily scooped up with *nivaley* (pieces) of roti or paratha, and delicious too! Sometimes, we have parathas stuffed with qeema. The crisp, flaky and steaming hot paratha with the intensely savoury-smelling cooked and *bhuna hua* (browned with gentle heat) qeema within it, is an absolute winner when it comes to winter brunches, either on its own with a dab of butter or with some mango pickle. Sometimes, Amma gets leftover cooked qeema filled inside well-seasoned mashed potatoes and fried like alu tikiyan or cutlets. The cutlets, unlike tikiyan, are, for some reason, teardrop-shaped rather than circular and are very popular. Another way this versatile preparation can be used is in qeema samosas. Amma often has what she calls *shaam ki chai* (like the English tradition of high tea) or sometimes get-togethers for Abba's literary friends or visitors to Aligarh. These small, triangular and much-loved snacks regularly make an appearance at these soirees. Raw qeema, of course, has a multitude of uses and is the precursor of many staple dinner items such as all manner of kebabs and koftey, including the unusual kache qeeme ke kebab—mince tenderized with unripe papayas, shaped into little patties and shallow fried. A papaya tree in your own garden is a very useful thing to have when making these, and the small, green, unripe papayas, the size of an orange, are a much-coveted item among neighbours.

Today, there are neither peas nor methi leaves in the kitchen, and Amma decides to have the qeema prepared with the berries, which are plentiful, flavourful, attractively coloured, and yet languish unloved in heavy bunches on the *jhaarh* or thorny bush. The berries are extremely sour, unlike the sweet and gloriously purple jamuns we love, the luscious and vibrant green ber or the juicy, delectable phalsa. We rue the fact that this sharp-tasting kakronda is not one of those berries that grows and lustily drapes itself on the walls with gay abandon, so we can eat them to our heart's content. If you bite into a kakronda, your face will crumple up like a scrap of paper destined for the waste bin. The berries are carefully picked, as there are vicious thorns to fend off and dodge, and rinsed under the hefty hand pump until they appear glistening and rosebud-like. Some are creamy white, while others are blush pink, like the cheeks of a newly-wed bride.

These berries are then painstakingly halved to scoop out the tiny but bitter seeds within, and cooked with the qeema. The spices and richness temper the tart berries, and in turn, the berries cut through the unctuousness of the mince, bringing forth a delicate balance and creating a dish that is pleasant to eat and behold and has great depth of flavour. The two essentially disparate and, in one case, overpowering and, in the other, downright unpleasant tastes come together as one, like two diverse and somewhat flawed singers joyously singing a mellifluous duet in full-throated harmony. This is food alchemy, like a conjuror's trick, and we witness it first-hand. There are appreciative murmurs as this creation is placed before us at dinner in a *donga*, or porcelain tureen, webbed with age, with a sprinkle of fresh coriander leaves on top. In no time at all, it is polished off along with some simple moong ki dal and roti.

While on the topic of dal, one day Amma casually announced that due to a family curse, she could not eat masoor ki dal while she was unmarried and could only do so after her marriage. We were bewildered on two accounts, actually. What was the rationale for this strange rule, and which one was actually masoor ki dal—the yellow one or the brown one? Up until that point, we had never given much thought to the specific names of dals, as 'dal' was simply dal. Usually yellow and porridge-like in consistency, sometimes it had spinach leaves mixed in it, and sometimes it was dry and not very dal-like in consistency, such as maash ki dal. Never the star of the show, always the supporting cast, along with roti or plain boiled rice (which in Amma's house was called khushka). Once masoor ki dal and its description had been clarified, we were eager to know about the curse. Did it apply to us as well? We wondered with dismay. Apparently, a seer had told an elder in the family that great misfortune would befall them if a Bakhsh girl ate masoor ki dal. She was from that family, and therefore it was strictly forbidden. She longed to eat that particular dal and could only eat it once she was married outside the clan, which was one of the first things she did when she got married. So it did not apply to us, which we were relieved to hear. As we contemplated this revelation, Amma remarked, 'Bechari Nanno, woh mehroom reh gayi, usne toh kabhi chakhi hi nahi.' This referred to her little sister, Nanno Nani, who unfortunately was married to a Bakhsh man and hence remained one even after marriage and so could never taste masoor ki dal, ever in her life! To this day, I think of this whenever I eat masoor ki dal and am thankful that no such restrictions exist for us or for our daughters.

Amma came from a very prosperous, progressive and well-established family, but perhaps in those days these beliefs could have been difficult to ignore. Her father (fondly addressed as Papa) was a Deputy Collector, an important post in those days. He was posted in different places, such as Allahabad, Banaras and Saharanpur. He also served as Wazir-e-Azam (Prime Minister) of Tonk. They, therefore, had a privileged upbringing, and she often regaled us with stories of her childhood, of living in a fabulous house with coloured mirror pieces adorning the walls and cornices, giving it the name of Sheesh Mahal, Papa's personal home, of angrezon ka zamana (during British rule) and the elegant social events of the time. Stories of glory and of loss, of joy and of sadness too. Her own mother died when she was only two years old, and after a while, a stepmother came who bore two sons. Amma was close to her little brothers, often mentioning Sabir and Chunnoo in her conversations, wistfully recalling their mischievous escapades. Sadly, both migrated to Pakistan at the time of Partition, and very little, if any, contact could be made with them for several years.

On a lighter note, Amma regales us with various folk songs she learned as a child. One that we absolutely adore because of its nonsensical, hilarious lyrics is:

Pajama pehna hath mein dastana samajh ke
Do bori matra kha gaye beedana samajh
Jootey se sharbat pee gaye paimana samajh ke
Donga bhar kaddu kha gaye sangdana samajh ke

(I wore pyjamas on my hands mistaking them for gloves
I had two sacks full of lentils mistaking them for quince fruit
I drank juice from a shoe mistaking it for a goblet
I ate a large bowlful of pumpkin mistaking it for chicken innards)

We also learned another delightful folk ditty, complete with exaggerated arm actions, about a hapless woman whose husband brought her some bajra, or pearl millets, to cook:

Mere jee ka jhanjhal mora bajra laya
Hai Allah qasam bajra hai Ram qasam bajra
Jab mai is bajre jo phatkan baithi
Urha urha jaye mora bajra sara

Jab mai is bajre ko kootan baithi
Phisal phisal jaye mora bajra sara
Hai Allah qasam bajra hai Ram qasam bajra

Jab mein is bajre ko goondhan baithi
Chipak chipak jaye mora bajra sara
Hai Allah qasam bajra hai Ram qasam bajra

(This pearl millet he got is giving me great grief
I swear upon Allah, I swear upon Rama
When I began to winnow the dough
It kept sticking to my hands)

Another sweet, slightly teasing song about a sleep-deprived, forgetful woman goes like this:

Chatank chhalla bhooliyai neend ki mari
Jab more sajan ne kangha manga
Mein jharoo pakraiyi, neend ki mari
Hamre balam ji hum hi ko maangein
Main jethani bethai aai neend ki maari

(I misplaced my precious ring as I hadn't slept
When my beloved husband asked for a comb I handed him a broom, as I hadn't slept
When my beloved husband called for me, I made my sister-in-law sit in my place, I hadn't slept)

And, of course, the 'Baingan song', which, in our opinion, made a huge fuss about a vegetable we collectively detested and turned our noses at. Did it really merit its very own song, we wondered?

Sakhi ri maine baingan do mol mangaye
Sakhi ri sun nandon ne baatein sunaiein
Sakhi ri sun sasu ne belan dikhaya
Sakhi ri sun devar ne munh bhi banya
Sakhi ri sun sayyan ne baarah phulke khaye
Ke baingan toh unko bahut hi bhaye
Badhey hi jatan se jo maine pakaye
Sakhi ri sun, baingain do mol mangaye

(O friend, I sent for two aubergines
My husband's sisters mocked me
My mother-in-law threatened me with a rolling pin
My little brother-in-law made a face
O friend, my husband had twelve rotis
O friend, he greatly savoured the aubergines
That I cooked with such care)

Another nonsense verse we enjoyed greatly was Hafiz Jalandhari's*
poem:

Kisi Sheher Mein Ek Tha Badshah

Kisi sheher mein ek tha badshah
Hamara tumhara khuda badshah
Magar badshah tha bahot hi ghareeb
Na aata tha koi bhi uske qareeb
Kiye ek din jama usne faqeer
Khilai unhe sone chandi ki kheer
Faqeeron ko phir jeb mein rakh liya
Ameeron wazeeron se kehne laga

---

* Urdu poet Hafiz Jalandhari (1900–1982) also wrote the ever-popular song 'Abhi
toh main jawan hoon', sung by Mallika Pukhraj.

Ki aao chalo aaj khelein shikar
Qalam aur kagaz ki dekhein bahaar
Magar hai samundar ka maidan tung
Karey kis tarah koi machhar se jung
Toh chiriya ye boli ki ai badshah
Karoongi mein apne chirey se byah
Magarmachh ko ghar mein bulaungi main
Samundar mein hargiz na jaungi main

(There lived a king in a city
Our almighty, the king
But the king was very poor
no one would come near
He gathered some paupers one day
And fed them gold and silver in pudding
He then put them in his pocket
He then called on the wealthy courtiers
And asked them to go hunting with him
Let's put pen and paper together
But the sea was not enough of a field
How can one do battle with a mosquito
So a bird told the king
I will marry my mate
I will invite the crocodile to my house
Never will I venture into the sea)

'Billo ka basta' is another sweet poem we memorized as children. In a lovely and symbolic way, with life coming full circle, my mother hand-knitted a Billo doll, complete with her own little satchel, and sent the poem for my daughter to read. So, it remains a much-loved poem in our house. Written by Ibne Insha,* it is about a little girl called Billo going to school with her bag. Below is the poem, followed by a translation by my daughter Alvira, then aged eleven or twelve.

> *Chhoti si Billo, chhota sa basta*
> *Thoonsa hai jisme kaagaz ka dasta*
> *Lakdi ka ghoda rooyi ka bhalu*
> *Chooran ki sheesha aalu kachalu*
> *Billo ka basta jin ki pitari*
> *Jab isko dekho pehle se bhari*
> *Lattu bhi isme rassi bhi isme*
> *Danda bhi isme gilli bhi isme*
> *Ai pyari Billo, yeh to batao*
> *Kya kaam karne iskool jaao*
> *Baahar nikalo yeh lakdi ka ghoda*
> *Ye lattoo, yeh rassi ye gilli danda*
> *Gudiya ke jootey jumper jurabein*
> *Bastey mein rakho apni kitabein*
> *Munh na banao iskool jaao*
> *Ai pyari Billo, ai pyari Billo*

> (Little Billo, with her little satchel
> Crammed inside is a bunch of papers
> A wooden horse, a teddy bear
> A bottle of chuuran, this and that
> It is like a genie's box

---

* Urdu poet, humourist and travel writer Ibn-e-Insha (1927–1978) also wrote the popular ghazal 'Kal chaudhwin ki raat thi', sung by Jagjit Singh, and 'Yeh baatein jhooti baatein', sung by Ghulam Ali.

It seems heavier every time you see it
It has a spinning top, a rope
It has a gilli-danda stick and a striker
O dear Billo, tell me this
What work do you do at school?
Take out this wooden horse
The spinning top, the rope and the gilli-danda
The doll's shoes, jumper and socks
Put your books in your bag
Don't make a face
O dear Billo, O dear Billo)

Amma had a very interesting life. As the wife of an esteemed and much-honoured scholar, she got to travel to far-off lands with him. She regaled us with her experiences in Chicago, Moscow and Rome. We listened with wide-eyed wonder about these fascinating places, the friends she made, the foods she ate and the magnificent sights she saw. We, as children, had never seen snow, so she described its texture and the crunchy sensation of it underfoot, wearing boots and a fur coat with an immaculately draped sari, much to our delight. She went everywhere with Abba and came back richer with the experience and knowledge gained, with a mind that was sharp as well as forward-thinking.

Coming back to the qeema kakronda, as in the circle of life, for everything that is missing in our lives, something new, fresh and unexpected makes an appearance. Sometimes it is pleasant, and sometimes it is not. Today, however, is one of those occasions when the unconventional and unprecedented become the precursors of the norm. The useless, neglected jhaarh-jhankaarh finally has a purpose, and a new dish is created.

Qeema Kakronda

250 gm minced mutton
25–30 kakronda berries, washed
2 medium onions, chopped
1 heaped tbsp ginger-garlic paste
1 tbsp coriander powder
½ tsp turmeric powder
½ tsp red chilli powder
salt to taste
2 tbsp oil
1 tsp garam masala
2 bay leaves
2–3 green cardamoms
2 whole green chillies
a few sprigs of fresh coriander leaves

Wash the mince well and drain. Keep aside.

In a heavy pot, heat the oil and brown the onions. Add the qeema and stir well.

Add the cardamom and bay leaves.

After a few minutes, add the ginger-garlic paste and spice powders and cook on low heat. You may need to add a little water to avoid the qeema sticking to the bottom of the pan and brown it gently. Add 1 cup of water, cover and cook.

Once almost cooked, add a slit green chilli and kakronda. Continue to cook until all the water is absorbed. Add salt to taste and sprinkle garam masala.

Take it out in a serving dish and sprinkle with chopped fresh coriander leaves and chopped green chillies.

Note: While growing up, I never saw anyone using readymade garam masala. This habit has stayed with me, and I prefer to grind small batches of whole spices and store them in an airtight container to use as needed. Back in the day, I am sure these were hand-pounded, but I use my trusty mini grinder! The difference in the depth of flavour and taste is unbelievable.

And, of course, on the subject of dal, here is a very popular and frequently made quick snack that Amma used to make.

Chana Dal ki Chaat

A firm favourite at the shaam ki chai, this provided a wholesome, spicy alternative to fried snacks and rich halwas.

2 cups chana dal
2 medium onions, finely chopped
1 tsp red chilli powder
4–5 green chillies, finely chopped
juice of a lemon
a pinch of rock salt
table salt to taste
a bunch of fresh coriander leaves

Soak the chana dal for 4–5 hours and bring it to a boil.

Cook until soft enough to be pressed between the fingers. Drain, and set aside.

Transfer the cooked dal to a large serving bowl. Add the chopped onions, green chillies, red chilli powder, rock salt, table salt and lemon juice. Gently mix.

Garnish with chopped coriander leaves and serve at room temperature.

~

Amma is the focal point of our childhood memories of Aligarh, and all else seems to happen in her vicinity, under her indulgent and watchful gaze, much like planets and asteroids circling the sun. Fittingly, the other women in the extended household have their own sparkle, but it is Amma who is undoubtedly the one with the magical stardust. To get to know them all and celebrate their uniqueness, generosity and warmth is the key to understanding the dynamics and the invisible glue that binds them all. Her own sister, whom we addressed as Nanno, Nanno's daughters, Azra Khala, who left for Canada after marriage, and Nasho Khala. On my mother's paternal side were the daughters of my nana's elder brother, Naseem Khala and Najma Khala. My Nana's sister's children included Ruqaiyya Khala. The wife of my Nana's younger brother, Shahida Chachi (our mother's aunt, but as they were similar in age, we called her Shahida Chachi too) was also part of the immediate family circle.

Wo itr daan sa lehja mere buzurgon ka
Rachi basi hai hui Urdu zabaan ki khushboo

—Bashir Badr

(The spoken words of my elders were like a bottle of perfume
The fragrance of Urdu language permeates through it)

Nasho Khala's Velvety Kofte

Nasho Khala lives nearby and comes over often. She is exuberant, affectionate and a lot younger than my mother (they are first cousins). She always has exciting news to share, and we listen with great fascination as she holds forth, her language heavily peppered with hilarious colloquialisms and idioms. We find her very entertaining and never tire of listening to her anecdotes, usually related to someone's wedding or visit. Her vocabulary is not erudite in the least, but it is rich in melodramatic expressions, similes and *muhawre*, or sayings, and is most unlike the conversations we have with one another. She is also an expert in singing traditional wedding songs and knows a multitude of them, which she sings in a *paatdaar* (powerful singing style) voice while playing the *dholak*. Most wedding songs in Western UP and perhaps other parts of India too are centred on the themes of jewellery, tackling a vicious mother-in-law or a bride's reluctance to leave her mother's home. They are purposefully worded in a rural UP dialect and evoke a simplistic bygone era where women stayed at home and coquettishly summoned their menfolk for various errands. One very popular song that Nasho Khala loves to sing, and we all love to join, goes something like this:

Mori chhalla si kamariya, naarha jhabbedar laiyyo . . . In which
the girl is asking her suitor or husband to bring her not just a
tasselled waistband for her delicate and slender waist but also
regional delicacies and sweets.

Tum sheher Bareilly jaiyyo, wahan se pedhe laiyyo
Khilaiiyo apne haath, naarha jhabbedar laiyyo

(Go to the city of Bareilly and fetch me pedhas
Feed them to me with your hands and bring my tasselled
waistband too)

And it goes on to include various other towns or cities of UP
famous for a particular mithai, such as Agra for petha, Banaras
for paan, Sandheela for laddoo and so forth.

The bride and bridegroom are referred to generically as
banno and *banna*, respectively.

While banno is a much admired, beautiful, delicate and
reticent figure in the songs, the banna can sometimes be childish
or churlish and is upbraided in verse form by the younger women
on the bride's side who humorously advocate on her behalf, so
she is granted luxurious gifts such as jewels and expensive finery.

In one such song, they urgently demand of the groom:

Jhumke kyun nahi laya banne jhumkon ki pukar hai
Yahin se mangwa de banne yahan bhi dukan hai
Doli darwaze khadi dulhan bhi tayyar hai . . .

(Why didn't you bring along earrings, the bride longs for them
You can quickly buy them from our local jeweller
The palanquin awaits the bride's departure; she is ready to
leave . . .)

This evokes a sense of urgency, playful manipulation of the forgetful groom, and outlines the shape of things to come. The bride must be pampered and cherished at all times; her mere wish is to be under his command. Often, these songs are set to the tune of popular Hindi film songs such as this one is set to the tune of '*Chup chup khadey ho zaroor koi baat hai, pehli mulaqat hai ji pehli mulaqat hai . . .*'* This makes it easier for others to join in and is greatly entertaining for all.

The playfully coquettish Hindi film song '*Kahin pe nigahein, kahin pe nishana*'† (from the film CID, 1956) is parodied as:

Dulhan meri shamma, dulha hai parwana
Jorha jo aaya toh woh bhi hai shahana,
Pehnegi (insert bride's name), *dekhega zamana*
Dhekho ji dekho nazar na lagaana

(My bride is a flame, her groom is a moth drawn to it
Fabulous clothes have been sent for her,
She will wear these for the world to see
Beware; do not cast an evil eye on her)

Another song echoes the thoughts and dreams of the bride, wistfully hoping her husband will always shower her with expensive jewellery to show his abiding love for her:

Nau man ka moti mala,
Saiyyan le aane wala

(A heavy pearl necklace,
And a husband who brings it to me)

---

* From the film *Badi Behen*, 1993.
† From the film *CID*, 1956.

The groom bringing jewellery and emphasizing the quantities of it, thus the generous heart, wealth and abiding love for his bride, is an ongoing motif in many of these songs:

Main kya janoon nausha mera aaya
Main kya kya janoon banna mera aya
Jhumkon ki jorhiyan wo rail bhari laya
Main kya . . .

(What do I know, my groom is here
What do I know, my groom is here
He has brought rail carriages full of earrings)

This emphasizes the quantity with railway carriages full of jewellery, sweets, clothing or even shoes—a ridiculous exaggeration.

The groom is subjected to more playful grilling by inquisitive and bold friends of the bride in this old ditty, making sure the groom stays on the straight and narrow path.

Aarha pajama, resham ka kamarbund bolo kahan gaye thhe
Pehli dupehri tumhe malan sang dekha
Haath liye gajra, bolo kahaan gaye the
Doosri dupehri tumhe dhoban sang dekha
Haath liye kurta, bolo kahaan gaye thhe . . .

(Dressed to the nines in your fancy trousers, where have been?
Have you been cavorting with the gardener's wife?
You had a string of flowers in your hand, where have you been?
The next afternoon, we saw you with washerwoman
You held aloft a tunic, where have you been?)

Another song extolls the beauty of the bride:

> Phoolon se nazuk, paanon se halki
> Tujhe phool kahoon ya paan, meri jaan

> (More delicate than flowers, lighter than a betel leaf
> What shall I call you—flower or a leaf, O dearest?)

The bride too can have a sassier, more militant avatar, especially when it comes to pitting her wits against the wily, often cruel mother-in-law, who is portrayed as a scheming, power-hungry harridan in these songs. In one such song, the bride resolves to keep her cool while dealing with the dreaded mother-in-law and humorously plans novel ways of dealing with her, addressing her groom and hinting at veiled threats. This one has no intentions of subservience or docility. All in good humour, of course!

> Ghabrana mat banne main toh nyari rahungi
> Teri amma se sau sau sawal karungi
> Vo ek toh main hazaar kahungi
> Uski dhoti ke tukde main chaar karungi
> Har tukde ke apne rumaal karungi

> (Don't worry, husband, I shall forever remain sweet
> I will ask your mother hundreds of questions
> If she says one thing to me, I will say a thousand
> I will rip her sari into pieces
> And make handkerchiefs for myself)

Some songs playfully target other relatives on the groom's side too. The sasur (father-in-law), devar (groom's younger brother), *nanad* (his sister) and in this case, the nanad's husband, the *nandoi*, who is the cherished *damaad* (son-in-law) of her new home and generally shown to be rather pompous, entitled and *robdar* (haughty), gets a grilling.

> *Pyare nandoya, sarota kahan bhool aayey*
> *Chhaila halwai se nazar lad gaiyan*
> *Mai bechari rabri khau donaa chaate saiyan*
> *Sarota kahan bhool aayey*
> *Pyare nandoya sarota kahan bhool aayey*

The forgetful nandoi, who has misplaced his trusted *sarota* (betel-nut cracker) is going from pillar to post—to a *halwai* (a seller of sweets), to a *rangrez* (one who dyes clothes or dupattas), to a *panwari* (paan-seller) and to a *sipahi* (policeman/guard), dragging along the family with him.

Another song, which has my favourite verse, rhapsodizes over the bride's friends, usually nubile maidens, who are also perhaps happily dreaming of the time when they will be the bride and the cynosure of all eyes . . .

> *Tujhe mehndi lagayingi wohi sakhiyaan*
> *Jinke gore gore haath, raseeli ankhiyan . . .*

(The girls who apply henna to your hands (o bride)
Will have fair hands and lustrous eyes . . .)

A beautiful wedding song that offers gentle words of advice and caution to take good care of the priceless jewels she has been entrusted with at such a young age. The girls were married fairly early in the olden days, and this song highlights the naivety, immaturity and innocence of the young bride:

Sejon pe bhooli chandanhaar, lath banno bheege itar main
Palang pe bhooli kangania, lath banno bheege itar main
Hariyali banno pehno jhumkey jatan se

(You forgot the exquisite necklace on the rose petals strewn on the marital bed
A lock of your hair found its way into a bottle of expensive perfume
And you left your bracelets on the bed, you are doused in perfume
O young bride, wear your earrings with great care)

Another song soulfully describes a young bride's predicament at *bidai* (departure from her parental home) with the words:

Mora leher leher jiya hoye re
Arey O ladley, darwaze ki chaukhat chhorh ke

(My heart is trembling
Whilst leaving the threshold of my home)

There is little or no dancing at our more traditional family weddings, but women sit on durries around the lead singer and clap and sing along. Some slightly risqué songs bring forth giggles and blushes from the bride-to-be. She sits on a low *chowki* (wooden chair) in the midst of her *maainyyo* ceremony, having been smeared and rubbed with a granular mixture of powders and herbs called *ubtan* that gently exfoliates the skin and makes it glow. She will later have intricate henna patterns drawn on her hands and feet. These patterns are floral motifs and geometric designs, and the bridegroom's initials are cleverly hidden in the patterns—a whimsical, sweet tradition. *Nakhh*, a resin, is burned on an open fire near her so that its heady perfume permeates in her pores, known as *nakhh basaana*. The exquisite and heavily embellished clothes stitched specially for her trousseau are arranged for all to admire. The complete set of an outfit is called a *jorrha* and includes the top and bottom half of the outfit with a matching dupatta. Most women in the family have helped get these ready on time. This includes the cutting and stitching of voluminous ghararas, hand-hemmed and made of gorgeous *kamkhab*, or brocade, or *poth* (pure, soft silk with gold thread, or *zari*, motifs woven into the weave). *Athlas* is a kind of silk material, with the embroidery done in coloured *resham*, or shiny threads, rather than zari. Poth comes in various designs; a *jaaldar* poth has an intricate lacy pattern covering a large surface of the cloth, like a curved network of interlinked patterns, like a beautiful trellis pattern. The other type is *booti wali* poth—a woven zari pattern of small patterns, repeated at regular intervals all over the cloth, leaving a greater expanse of the silk fabric bare. These could be geometric or paisley-patterned and sometimes small dot-like circular designs known *asharfi* poth.

These are cut in a meticulous and elaborate manner, the precious fabric carefully laid out flat on the chowki, sharp scissors making a *khach-khach* sound, interspersed with directions and comments from the women involved in this task. The seams of the *kaliyan* that make the *gowt*, or gathered lower half, are set at a diagonal, so the fall of the fabric is also at an *aureb*, or angle, rather than straight down. This gives a flowing, flared look that ghararas are famous for. The upper part of the gharara falls straight and is called a *paat*, making sure the *kamarband* threaded through the *nefa*, or waistband, usually a sturdy though fine red cotton material known as *tuul*, does not bulge at the navel. The ghararas come in every conceivable colour and a plethora of patterns. The style of ghararas can be traditional, with the top and bottom halves being made from the same material with a seam demarcating them at the level of the knees. A delicate golden or silver lace is carefully hand-sewn over this seam. Then there are the more elaborate *chatapatti* ghararas, made of tiny diamond-shaped pieces or *tukrhhiyan* of different coloured silk fabric, stitched painstakingly together in a patchwork of contrasts that forms the fabric of the bottom half of the gharara. Sometimes these pieces could be shaped like fish scales or squares. To join these pieces together is like doing a giant jigsaw puzzle and requires a lot of patience and attention to detail. Sometimes, sequins or *sitarey* are hand sown on the seams of the individual pieces for extra refinement and splendour, or delicate karchob embroidery or even *kaamdani* (beautiful patterns made with tiny pieces of flattened metal strips to look like metallic studs) is done along the seams. The colours of a chatapatti are usually jewel-bright, with a matching dupatta dyed in various colour blocks, complementing the gharara. The qameez or the blouse is generally one colour. Most people wear a fitted qameez in plain silk, matching with the gharara and reaching a mid-thigh level, while others are partial to a kurti in a soft, flowing fit. Another type of gharara is the *farshi*, which trails behind the wearer, much like the train of a western bridal gown. It is usual to elegantly drape the trailing end around one's forearm for a regal and begum-worthy silhouette, especially while walking. We watch with awe as these gorgeous outfits, which started life as a *thaan* of material bought for the occasion, or carefully treasured over the years, take on unbelievably stunning incarnations. The matching dupattas have elaborate *takan* (golden or silver edging or lace), are lovingly hand-hemmed (*turpai*) and are either embroidered in sinuously curving fronds and branches of flowers and buds or have kaamdani. Some bridal dupattas are edged with a tinsel lace called *kiran*, either in silver or gold, or a kaarchob edging. There are intense and deep discussions on the type of *takan-kalabattoo*, strands of resham and zari, twined together to make a ribbon like lace, *paimaq, gota, lachka* and *jhalar*, the overhanging edging. The leftover silk or brocade finds its use in a home-made matching purse with a drawstring, known as a *batua*. Not a scrap of the precious, expensive and exquisite cloth goes to waste. The more industrious women will also eke out a dainty pair of matching slippers or *jootis*, of course strictly for indoor wear!

Another job we youngsters get is to fill little cloth bags or metal containers with *bari* goodies. These usually contain nuts and dried fruit and are distributed to wedding guests. Metal containers are often lidded bowls with the bride and groom's names and the wedding date inscribed on them. We all sit amidst mounds of walnuts, almonds, cashew nuts, raisins and the all-important chhuarey and misri (little chunks of crystallized sugar) and set about filling up the bags or bowls. There are also vast *seenis* of mithai for everyone to eat and to be sent to neighbours and friends. The bride-to-be will be fed by her friends or sisters once her hands are decorated with henna (mehndi). There will be yakhni pulao, shami kebab and hari dhaniye ki chutney or something similar for the Mehndi Lunch. Back in the day, when mehndi did not come in polythene cones and was hand-ground using henna leaves, an absent-minded uncle was caught off-guard with hilarious consequences at one of the family weddings. The henna paste had been placed near the kitchen in a large serving bowl. He helped himself to a large spoonful of mehndi paste over his already piled-up plate of food, thinking it to be chutney and only realized his error when he sat down to eat his meal! Even to this day, the memory of that incident makes us all giggle.

Wedding meals are elaborate affairs, as guest lists run into the hundreds. There is either a shamiana in an open field, near the house or a suitable enclosed space or hall is hired. A highly recommended and reputable outside caterer who is familiar with the requirements of wedding feasts is on the job. Lengthy discussions about the menu take place. On the day of the actual wedding, vast vats of food arrive, the smells of which permeate the entire neighbourhood. The food is sumptuous, including usually three or four meat-based saalan, including the omnipresent qorma, bhuna gosht and murgh musallam. Accompanied by extravagantly prepared biryani, seekh kebabs, freshly made tandoori roti, sheermal, rumali roti and several desserts known collectively as meetha. These could be hot, syrupy and succulent gulab jamun, vibrantly coloured and richly flavourful zarda pulao or my personal favourite, gulatthi.

Gulatthi is a dessert that surpasses all, in my opinion. It is similar to firni but is a lot creamier, thicker and more luxurious in every way. A wedding feast without gulatthi is a disappointment and a grave error, without doubt. It has been savoured at millions of Aligarh weddings, formal dinners and other special celebrations over the years. Something that is greatly looked forward to as a perfect end to a sumptuous celebratory meal, the decadent qormas, sheermal and pulaos, to a sensory backdrop of rustling silks, brocades, jangling bangles and gold *kangans* (bracelets), an intense smell of rose petals and the murmurs of social niceties. The special earthenware *matkis*, or pots, hide within them the most delectable flavours in a rich kheer-like texture, redolent with coconut, cardamom and a plethora of dried fruits and nuts. The matki gives it the most wondrous aroma and taste. Of course, one tears off the rani-pink kite paper, almost friable and yielding easily to the merest tug to sink into this sublime and unique creation.

An institution in itself, the recipe has been carefully and painstakingly handed down from the cooks that provide catering at these functions. I am not sure if it is made at home as much as kheer is. A variety of mithai and halwas are served at weddings. Made with milky khoya, grains of various kinds, even lentils, imbued with the aromatic and decadent base of asli ghee, copious amounts of sugar and nuts; these are not for the faint-hearted and most certainly not for those watching their waistlines! Sohan halwa is one such heavenly concoction: the warming, dark-hued and unctuously chewy squares that melt in the mouth and are a special addition to any wedding feast. A Rampuri wedding feast is, for certain, incomplete without one, but it does make an appearance in our local weddings at times, thanks to visiting relatives and friends.

At a previous wedding, the baraat came from a place in Hardoi called Sandeela. There was much excitement and hushed murmurs about the famed Sandeele ke laddoo, reaching fever pitch in the build-up to the wedding. I am not sure if anyone even remembers the gharara of the bride or the name of the groom, but these laddoos are imprinted in our minds. Tiny and perfectly formed with a melt-in-the-mouth texture, they come in small matkis or earthenware pots that have four or five of these laddoos, and the pots are sealed with a fine red paper. Made with khoya, ghee and sugar, these have a delicate yet earthy flavour and are irresistible.

There are many exciting and traditional rituals at our weddings. The *nikah*, or wedding, itself is a solemn and brief ceremony, consisting mainly of consents from the bride and groom in the presence of witnesses. The merriment comes in the form of rituals such as *joota churai*, *aarsi musaf* and a few others. Aarsi musaf is the quintessential traditional ritual, harking back to the day when the bride and groom first set their eyes on each other on the actual wedding day! Such is the necessity to maintain the purdah that the blushing bride, rather than gaze at her groom directly, steals a look at a reflection of his face in an ornate ring with a round piece of mirror set in its centre. This ring, usually larger than the average ring, is often made of *kundan* (pure gold) or set with precious stones. Traditionally, the groom says out loud, 'Aap meri dulhan aur main aapka ghulam' (You are my bride and I am your servant), met by much applause from the girl's side. A large and ornate *odhni* (dupatta) is held over the bride and groom, shielding them from prying eyes and cocooning them in a blessed space. In the present day, this ritual seems anachronistic, almost obsolete, but is still practised, at times replaced with a florally decorated or bejewelled hand-held mirror for the groom to gaze at his bride. A copy of the holy Quran is placed alongside the newly-weds to bless them in their onward marital life and keep them safe in their journey together.

Towards the end of the evening, there is a tearful and emotionally charged *rukhsati*, where the bride bids farewell to her home and family. The bride accompanies her groom, led by his family, and the bride's family trails behind, tearful and forlorn. A copy of the holy Quran is held just above her head by a member of her family as she makes this highly emotional and special journey, leaving the safe confines of her parental home and stepping into an unknown world. Leaving behind loved ones, familiar faces, childhood friends, girlish dreams and pastimes, and stepping into womanhood, a life of dignified adulthood, responsibility, being in unfamiliar and slightly different environs, and becoming part of a new family. The next day is the *walima*, or the reception hosted by the groom's family, with yet another sumptuous banquet. An older ritual in Amma's time was the *sarasari*, an appendage to the *ghoonghat* (bridal veil). It was an ornate headpiece, embellished with gold beads and made with red or green satin. Amma tells us hers had solid gold asharfis, or gold coins, sewn on to it. It comes from the bridegroom's side, the sasural, and once it is taken off, a special prayer for blessing, or *niyaz*, is done.

The bride visits her family on the *chauthi* (fourth day) as a married woman along with her new husband. A special, elaborate outfit, or jorha, is earmarked well in advance for this visit. The bride is resplendent in her jewellery, *suhagan* (bridal) red and green glass bangles and mehndi, and there is a lavish feast in her honour, just for the close family members and elders of her family. Over the years, we have attended many weddings of cousins, young aunts and uncles and others in the extended family, spread across the length and breadth of UP. The prospect of dressing up in our finery, the outstanding food and the chance to catch up with family, many of whom we do not see that often, are all factors in motivating us to attend as and when we can. Some weddings stand out in our memory for their unusual and amazing entertainment, like the spirited qawwali singers at Munne Mamu's wedding in Badayun singing *Unke paon mein mehndi lagi hai, aane jaane ke qabil nahin hain* (She has henna applied on her feet, she is unable to venture out), but food is an important benchmark too. Tayyab Mamu's son's wedding had one of the best feasts we remember. As baraatis, we are strewn with rose petals, sprinkled with rose water from elegant and ornamental *khaasdaans*, or silver urns, and given a *gajra*, or roses threaded on a piece of string. Some wore them like bracelets, and some of us wore them in our hair. The traditional multi-coloured fabric *qanaats* (cloth screens) held up by wooden poles, the entire Sota Mohulla (the locality where my mother's family comes from) gathered around, and people in sherwanis, achkans and ghararas milled about. The air was redolent with the heady and tantalizing fragrance of roses and the aroma of biryani . . .

Today, Nasho Khala has brought with her a *donga*, or tureen, of koftey—her specialty. Koftey are little balls of minced mutton. Submerged in gravy, they are a family favourite. Each kofta is a delectable, delicately spiced and succulent morsel, individually shaped by hand. Sakina had already prepared turai ki sabzi, arhar ki dal and a large stack of rotis for lunch. We will now sit down at the chowki, amidst various threads of conversations running in parallel, and eat this feast that is laid out in front of us. The rotis are wrapped in an old muslin cloth, so they remain soft and warm. They are kept in a battered and worn wicker basket referred to as 'dallia' (with a hard D sound, not to be confused with broken wheat dalia or porridge!). There is a *surahi* nearby and several glasses for people to help themselves to cool, fresh water from this earthenware pitcher with a narrow neck. And even though I have never met her, as she was my great-great-great aunt, it reminds me of an ancestor known as Surahi Dadi. She was the sister of my mother's grandmother, called Surraiyya, and was nicknamed Surahi by all who knew her. She had a beautiful, slender and elegant swan-like neck, with, as legend goes, smooth as marble, translucent and fair skin on her neck so much so that when she drank water, you could see its passage down the neck . . .

People sit cross-legged on the massive chowki or spread out on the numerous chairs scattered around. The conversations continue, uninterrupted by TV, radio or any other distractions. The meal is eaten, and the dishes are cleared away. Nasho Khala looks pleased. There are hardly any koftey remaining. Everyone murmurs about how *makhmali* (velvety) and *mazedar* (flavoursome) they were. Nasho Khala, in her characteristic comical manner, waves off the volley of compliments with a rural inflection to her voice and a self-effacing 'Aye na . . . chalo hato, koi aisa murgh-mutanjan bhi na tha!' (It was nothing special or elaborate.)

Makhmali Koftey

For the koftey or meatballs:
250 gm fine minced meat
1 tsp garlic-ginger paste
1tsp khus-khus (poppy seeds)
½ tsp garam masala
2 tbsp besan (chickpea flour)
¼ tsp salt

For the gravy:
1 tbsp ginger-garlic paste
½ tsp turmeric powder
½ tsp red chilli powder
2 tbsp coriander powder
2 tbsp cooking oil
2 medium onions, chopped
2 tbsp plain curd or yoghurt
a sprig of coriander leaves for garnish

To make the gravy, heat the oil in a heavy-bottomed pot and fry the chopped onions till browned.

With a slotted spoon, take the browned onion out on a plate and set it aside to crisp up.

In the same oil, on a gentle heat, cook the ginger-garlic paste along with the spice powders and a splash of water to prevent burning. Stir it continuously and wait for the oil to separate, which usually takes about 10 minutes.

Add the curd and garam masala, stirring continuously to avoid lumps. Crumble the crispy onions into the mix. Add a glass of water and let it simmer.

Meanwhile, make the koftey. Gently roast the besan on a flat pan or tawa till you can smell an earthy, nutty aroma. It should not brown or burn.

In a bowl, mix the minced meat and all the other ingredients, including the roasted besan, by hand and shape them into lemon-sized balls.

Gently add these balls to the gravy, one by one. Add another cup of water and cook for 20 to 30 minutes on a very low heat, letting it gently simmer.

Do not stir, lest the koftey break; rather, gently lift and sway the pot once or twice. Check the seasoning.

Once in the serving tureen, sprinkle with fresh chopped coriander leaves.

~

Weddings and feasts are closely intertwined, and we have had some memorable feasts in extremely convivial surroundings at most of these family weddings, dressed in our ghararas, bangles and jewellery. There are countless photographs, mostly taken by Mamu rather than an official photographer or an outsider, as these capture the essence of the very special and gloriously joyful moments. The wedding videos—those black rectangle-shaped VHS tapes—were more a part of our own weddings later on. These too were watched countless times, and each time they proved more entertaining than before as newer, exciting activities were discovered in the background. Again, the aunts, cousins and elders were an important part of the uninhibited and gleeful revelry at these occasions.

Mahak rahi hai zameen chandni ke phoolon se
Khuda kisi ki mohobbat pe muskurya hai

—Bashir Badr

(The earth is fragrant with the moonlight from the flowers
The Almighty has smiled at someone's love)

Abba's Favourite Kali Gajar ka Halwa

Shahreyar Mamu is visiting for his elevenses. A much-acclaimed poet, he is not related to us by blood but is like a son to Amma and a close friend of our Badey Mamu. He is a keen foodie who enjoys cooking as well. His qeema dopiyaza is legendary, and anyone fortunate enough to taste it can never forget its sheer perfection and sublime excellence. He is soft-spoken and likes his tea without milk and with only a slice of lemon. His tea is brought in while he converses with Abba. They mostly talk about books and poetry. Abba has his usual milky, sweet tea. The tray is a beautifully engraved Moradabadi one with upturned, sinuously curved handles. On it is a delicate, embroidered tray cover made of muslin. Amma loves to embroider roses, and there is a small and pretty bunch of vivid red roses with mossy green leaves at each corner and a white hand-crocheted *bael*, or lace, edging the tray cloth.

Amma refers to the Victorian art of crochet as 'krushiya'. She is skilled and prolific, embroidering almost every article of household linen and making elaborate and multi-coloured crochet-knit caps, purses, ponchos and even shawls (by joining together multitudes of tiny, biscuit-sized squares made with leftover scraps of wool). I have never shown any interest in learning these exquisite crafts, but my older sister is a willing and proficient pupil. Coming back to the tray, there are two dainty glass bowls (part of a set she received when she got married). They are made of a delicate, greenish-tinged glass with a pale hand-painted floral motif on its outer aspect and a dull gold finish on the rim. Over the years, careless handling by inept maids has dwindled the number, and only a few of these remain, supplemented by thick and sturdy, 'cut-glass look' ones that are cheap and cheerful and used for '*aaye-gayey*', or humdrum, ordinary people. There are small, ornate, silver-coloured spoons speared obliquely in the halwa that these bowls contain, like an old-fashioned quill in a pot of ink. This is halwa, but not any old halwa. This is kali gajar ka halwa, something that Abba adores. He loves to recite an old folk song: '*Kala laya re, kali gajar ka halwa . . .*' and eagerly awaits the short-lived season during which purple carrots are sold at vendors. When they do arrive, Sakina promptly snaps up a few kilos so they can be washed, peeled, grated and cooked into this luscious and unique treat for Abba. It requires meticulous cooking with ghee and sugar over a low flame, so it is 'bhuna', holding its shape, moist but not wet, completely cooked but not a watery sludge. The knobbly, coarse-looking, almost other-worldly purple carrots do not look promising in their natural state, but then this is about the finesse and skill with which they are cooked. The resultant halwa is a deep, dark and rich purple colour with amethyst-coloured strands weaving through it, an exquisitely flavoured delicacy, earthy and bold yet tantalizingly exotic, offset with a contrasting sprinkling of crumbled khoya (dried whole milk) and blanched almond flakes, like stars and stray clouds amongst an inky winter sky. Both Abba and Shahreyar Mamu savour it greatly and murmur appreciatively.

Abba and Amma at home (Professor Ale
Ahmed Suroor and Zahida Suroor)

Amma wearing beautiful traditional jewellery
and a crinkled (*chuna*) dupatta

Amma and Abba—sunshine days and the trusty transistor

Amma and Abba—Abba looking handsome in his black sherwani and
Amma in a *gharara*

Amma as an elegant and doting grandmother

Amma in her youth

Mohammadi Begum (Amma's stepmother) with
her baby son Sabir

Amma with her beloved newspapers—a habit
that remained till the very end

Amma wearing a net dupatta and a cotton chikan kurta, paired most probably with a chintzy cotton gharara for daily wear

Amma reading

Nasho Khala (second from left) with Amma
and some other relatives

My parents after their wedding—Mummy
in her bridal gharara, *jhoomar* and *teeka*

Abba with Amma at home

Abba with his father, Maulvi Karam Ahmed

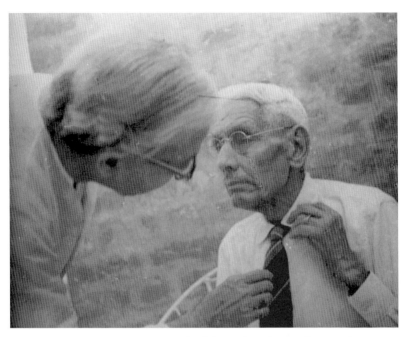

Abba with Amma's father (Papa), his father-in-law, the very dapper Rehman Baqsh Qadri

Abba at home with his sculpture

One of numerous letters from Abba to me

Abba on a wintry afternoon at the Aligarh home

An antique paandan

A dastarkhwan

Abba at the university

Abba with the writer Qurratulain Hyder

My parents at their wedding

(L-R) Abbu, Abba and Mummy

(L-R) Amma, Abba, Mummy and
Azra Khala

Mummy surrounded by her family at her wedding
Top row: Amma's younger brother Chunnu,
Amma, Abbu, Amma's father, Mummy,
Muhammadi Begum, Abba
Bottom row: Zohra Khala, Azra Khala, Tariq Mamu

Naseem Khala

Naseem Khala with Amma—a more
recent picture

Tasneem and Qaiser Khala standing,
her daughter Farzana between
Abba and Amma

Dastarkhwan meals; Abba visiting friends in Kashmir in 1940

Abba's younger brother Aulad Ahmed

Amma, Mummy, Azra Khala (Nanno's
elder daughter)

Mummy and Azra Khala as young girls
on a swing in Sawan

Najma Khala (standing, left) with her husband and baby (Babur) Sitting: Tai (Amina), Tau (Ibne Ahmed), Maulvi Karam Ahmed, Abba

Tai (Amina), Tau (Ibne Ahmed), Maulvi Karam Ahmed, Abba

Baramdah: Chhote Mamu and Mummy standing, Abba and Amma sitting.
Her trusty sewing machine can be seen.

Aligarh, Numaish

Nanno with her sisters Amma and Zohra Khala

Me as a child in Aligarh

Urdu poetry, or shayari, is the topic of conversation, and both speak in soft, measured tones. I am sitting in the courtyard nearby, ensconced in a comfy chair, reading a book. The dappled winter sunshine is comforting and uplifting. There is a mushaira being organized, and Abba and Shahreyar Mamu have been invited to grace the occasion. A mushaira is a gathering of esteemed poets who each recite their works, new and old, to a rapt audience that expresses its appreciation with cries of *Waah!* and *Bahot Khoob!* We all subsequently attend the mushaira that is held locally and greatly enjoy the experience. The witty exchanges between the poets and the lively interaction, both amongst the poets and members of the audience, are an extremely new, albeit delightful, concept for us. On the way back, Abba patiently explains the meanings of some verses that we didn't understand and also the finer aspects of poetry writing in Urdu, including the meters of rhythm and the various kinds and forms of poetry. We note the *takhallus*, or nom de plume, of various participating poets and also of great poets in the past. Some, like Abba, have a singular name, in his case, Suroor, which means intoxication (he is a teetotaller, so this is very ironic!), Hali (Altaf Hussain) or the iconic poet Ghalib (Mirza Asadullah Baig). Some poets have a second part of their takhallus that indicates their provenance, such as Josh Malihabadi, Jigar Muradabadi, Waseem Barelvi and Shakeel Badayuni.

On many a leisurely evening, after dinner, a session of bait-bazi is held at our grandparents' home. Akin to the popular Indian games of Antakashari (with film songs) or Atlas (based on geography), this contest involves the consecutive recitation of an Urdu couplet, or sher, that begins with the letter the previous sher ended with, thus forming a chain of seemingly unrelated shers. These could be the popular or well-known ones, such as those by Ghalib, Iqbal or Faiz, which we were all familiar with, or the more obscure ones that served their purpose when one was stuck with an awkward letter to start with. The teams usually included a mix of adults and the younger lot, and it was a spirited, highly competitive team game. Many a time, when faced with a difficult letter, a wily player sought to 'modify' an existing sher to fit in with the demand. Abba's adjudication was the final word on these occasions, and the errant player was booed and mercilessly teased. An invalid or incorrect sher was termed *alqat*—an embarrassment to endure. Most of the shers were of an erudite quality and were well respected in the world of poetry; however, a few scatological or puerile ones made their way, courtesy *Diwan-e-Chirkeen.** We were amazed at the sheer depth of knowledge and recall of our mother, the aunts and others participating. It was customary to start the game with Bismillah (in the name of Allah, the opening verse from the Quran, and also said when starting something, to be blessed). As the entire line is *Bismillah ir Rehman ir Rahim* (Allah, the merciful and compassionate), the first player has to start with the letter Meem of the Urdu alphabet, or the M sound.

Typically, this sher would be:

Muddai lakh bura chahey toh kya hota hai
Wahi hota hai jo manzoor-e-khuda hota hai

(The adversary may wish great misfortune upon you, it will not matter
What God wills, happens ultimately)

In the Urdu script this ends with the 'Yae' alphabet
Hence, the second sher could be:

---

* Sheikh Baqar Ali 'Chirkeen' was an Urdu poet known for his scatological poetry. His collected works include *Diwan-e-Chirkeen.*

Yeh na thi hamari qismat ke visal e yar hota
Agar aur jeetey rehte yahi intezar hota

(It was not my fortune that I would be united with my beloved
If I had lived further, I would have continued to wait)

And this would be followed by something like:

Aankh se dur na ho dil se utar jayega
Waqt ka kya hai guzarta hai guzar jayega

(When one is away from sight, they may get forgotten
As for time, it passes and will pass)

And so, it continued until a player or team got stuck or was disqualified.

It was not only a great pastime; it also enriched our knowledge and understanding of Urdu shayari and was a good family activity as we sat around leisurely in our courtyard, on various chairs, cushions and chowkis, whiling away time together.

Abba would sometimes sing me lullabies to put me to sleep. Only they were passages from the poet Iqbal's wonderful poetry. Sometimes, '*Sitaron ke aagey*', sometimes '*Shikwa*', or my favourite, '*O ghaafil Afghan*'. Even though I never read Iqbal as an adult, I can recite them faultlessly just from the childhood memory of listening to Abba in his gentle, undulating voice.

Another form of expressing oneself poetically was to write a *sehra*, a paean and celebratory message for the groom-to-be. It extols the virtue of the groom, and prays for joyful wedded bliss for the newly-weds. Abba wrote a special one for many in the family, including my brother, and it is a very special keepsake to cherish and possibly frame and display. In many weddings in UP, it was customary for the sehra, usually penned by a well-read and poetically inclined elder in the family, a local poet or a family friend, to be printed on the thin paper napkins that were placed at the tables for guests at the wedding feasts. Printed simply in Nastaleeq script in black ink, they invariably had decorative, colourful floral borders and the poet's name at the end, along with the wedding date. A similar poetic message for the girls in the family getting married would be a joyful Mehndi or an emotionally charged Rukhsati. Abba wrote these for his daughter (our mother) and for us all when it was our time, and we still cherish those precious and unique lines, written specially for us.

The rukhsati written by him for our mother was as follows:

Mahjabeen ki Rukhsati (A Rukhsati for Mahjabeen)

Beti nayi fizaein teri muntazir hein ab
Tujhko bula rahein hain nazare naye naye
Apni toh had yahi thi ab aagey ki rah hai
Manzil nayee hai hongey isharey nayey nayey
Maanoos baam o dar mein bhi ek baat hai magar
Dekh aasman naya hai sitare naye naye
Ain e zeest kya hai? Faqat zauq inqalab
Har gaam par hain iskey isharey nae nae

—Suroor (1959)

(O Daughter, new horizons await you
New vistas beckon you

Our path together has come to an end, yours is ahead of you
You will have new goals and signposts
As you leave the familiar surroundings behind
New skies and stars are yours
What is the principle of Life? It is to bring about a change
At every step you will find new signposts to guide you)

A delightfully humorous and evocatively titled poem, 'Shubh Gharhi' (auspicious moment, in Hindi), was penned by Abba on the occasion of my sister's wedding many years ago. It recreates those special and beautiful moments so vividly that it seems like one is present and in the midst of the joviality and celebration that marked the happy occasion. Many relatives had come from other parts of India and abroad to attend, and there was bustling activity and joy all around:

Shubh Gharhi (Auspicious Moment)

Rakhshi ke aqd ki jo qareeb aaee Shubh Gharhi
Batne lagi nishat ki daulat gharhi gharhi
Gayey saheliyon ne barhe josh se wo geet
Zohra falak se wajd mein aakar nikal parhi
Dulha dulhan ke sholae rukhsar kay tufail
Lagta hai jaise bazm mein chhooti ho phuljharhi
Kya khoob tha wo joota churaney ka khel bhi
Chhoti baraat walon se kya chaumukhi larhi
Tabi ka pairahan bhi tha kya bolta hua
Us par nazar parhi toh usi par rahi parhi
Lotey wuzu ke wastey Urfi ne rakh diye
Yeh aur baat hi ke zaroorat nahi parhi
Wo muskura rahe thhe Suroor aur Jalil bhi

Chhupti nahi chhupane se ashkon ki ab larhi
Har simt chhut rahi thi lateefon ki phuljhari
Naati bhi khush thhe aur barati bhi shad thhe
Madham phawar si bhi hai mausam bhi hai khushgawar
Parhne ne paye zameen boondein barhi barhi
Dulha dulhan ke wastey karte thhe sab dua
Aae na inki zeest mein saat koi karhi

(The auspicious moment of Rakhshi's wedding is here
The joyousness is being spread all around
Her friends are singing special songs
There is laughter all around
The flushed cheeks of the bride and groom
Are like sparking fireworks
The ritual of hiding the groom's shoes was delightful
Chhoti (youngest sister) drove a hard bargain with the groom's
side (for the return of the shoes)
Tabi's (sister/me) attire was stunning
It was very eye-catching
Urfi (brother) thoughtfully provided lotas for ablutions
However, they were not needed in the end
The bride's father and maternal grandfather stood smiling
But they were unable to stop their tears
Humour and laughter were everywhere
The bride's and groom's sides were both happy
The weather was pleasant, there was a gentle drizzle too
Soon there were bigger raindrops too
All the guests prayed for the bride and groom
So that troubles stay away from their marital life together)

This poem captures the day so beautifully, with all its cheer, quirks and loveliness.

Of course, we did not have to wait to be grown up and get married to have a very special poem just for us. A simple yet endearingly sweet poem that Abba wrote for us four siblings when we were young was as follows:

Chaar Yaar (My Four Friends)

Number ek, barha hi nek
Khaye cake, piye milk shake
Number do, kahe ro ro
Mujhe bhi do, mujhe bhi do
Number teen, barhi miskeen
Bajaey been, jayey cheen
Numbar char, barhi hoshiyar, abhi phulwar, abhi talwar
Humari yaar, humari yaar

(Child number one is good of heart
He eats cake, drinks milkshake
Child number two wails
And wants it too
Poor child number three
Plays a flute and goes to China
Child number four is clever and impetuous
But she's my friend, she's my friend)

The first grandchild, my brother Urfi, got his own poem when he was a baby, long before the arrival of us sisters:

Urfi

> Yoon toh bacchey aur bhi hain
> Lambey aur chaukor bhi hain
> Urfi ki kya baat bhaai, Urfi ki kya baat . . .

> (There are many other children
> Of various shapes and sizes,
> There is none like Urfi, there is none)

His own first born, Siddiq, our Badey Mamu, had a poem specially written by him for his first birthday:

Pehli Salgirah (First Birthday)

> Nanhey miyan ki saalgirah ki khushi hai aaj
> Yeh bazm bazm e aish o massarat bani hai aaj
> Laatee hain aasman se wo nikhatein hawa
> Shadab jinke faiz se har har kali hai aaj
> Pheekey hain jink e samnejalwe bahaar ke
> Dekho hamari bazm main wo chandni hai aaj
> Daade hai shad shaad toh dadi hain bagh bagh
> Ma baap ke labon pe hansee khilti hai aaj

> (The little master's birthday brings joy today
> This gathering has become one of joy and festivities
> The breeze brings a sweet fragrance from the skies
> Each bud blooms to its fullest today
> the splendour of the spring season seems dull in comparison
> to the bright moonlight in our midst, oh look

his grandfather is joyful, his grandmother is ecstatic
His parents have smiles on their faces)

Abba regularly writes in his journal. He shows us an entry:

*Apney nawasey Urfi aur apni nawasiyon Rakhshanda, Tabinda aur
Zarine Taj ke naam:*

(For my grandson Urfi and my granddaughters Rakhshanda,
Tabinda and Zarine Taj)

It is a dedication to us in the words of his favourite poet, Iqbal.
This is from his beautiful nazm, '*Saqi Nama*'.

Merey deeda-e-tar ki bekhwabiyan
Mere dil ki poshida betabiyan
Mere nala-e-neem shab ka niyaz
Mere khilwat-o-anjuman ka gudaaz
Umangein meri aarzooein meri
Umeedein meri justjuein meri
Meri fitrat aina e rozgar
Ghazalan e afkar ka marghzar
Mera dil meri razm gah e hayat
Gumaanon ke lashkar yaqeen ka sabaat
Yahi kuchh hai saqi mata e faqir
Issi se faqiri mein hoon mein amir
Mere qafiley mein luta de issey
Luta de thikane laga de isse

(The sleeplessness of my tear-laden eyes
the hidden restlessness of my heart

the supplications to my grief at midnight
The merging of my solitude and social existence
My longings, my wishes
My hopes and quests
My disposition is a mirror of the times.
A pasture for the gazelles of ideas
My heart, the tribulations of life
The uncertainties, doubts and steadfastness of belief
O Saqi (cup-bearer), this the true wealth of a pauper
And that is why I am rich despite my poverty.
Distribute it amongst my dear ones
Give it away, let it be of use to them)

We feel very special, even more so when he patiently explains to us the meaning of these beautiful lines. The complex words and deep metaphors come alive, each phrase pulsating with emotions, imagery and exquisite lyricism. We are entranced.

There are two things of vital importance to Abba—poetry and paan! He loves his fresh paans to the extent that they had to be mailed to him when he was abroad. The paan, or betel leaf, is palm-sized, roughly heart-shaped and has its own paraphernalia tailored to the needs of the person eating it. In Amma's home and many others that we visited, it was customary to have a *paandan* actively in use. This was an ornate metal case with a hinged lid and several little compartments inside for the various accompaniments. These included *kattha choona*, *chhaliya* and *tambakhoo* in a tiny glass bottle. Kattha is catechu paste, reddish brown in colour, and it imparts the characteristic blood-red colour to the mouth of the one chewing paan. Choona is simply a paste of slaked lime that is very astringent and strong in flavour. Chhaliya is a carefully chopped areca nut, a brown marble-sized nut with cream striation inside and a smooth cappuccino-coloured exterior, quite similar to nutmeg in appearance. Amma would meticulously chop these with her *sarota*, a plier-like, highly ornate metallic cutting instrument. When Amma used her sarota, it sounded like a Morse code message, with a series of sounds and pauses, producing a mound of lentil or grain-sized tiny pyramids in a short period of time. All these were in their little compartments and were regularly replenished. A pair of dainty scissors was also specifically kept inside to snip off the stems and pointy ends of the paan. It was then divided into two equal halves and smeared carefully with the kattha and choona.

Abba was partial to a desi paan. In addition, he had a portable *dibbiya* that he carried everywhere, whether he was visiting friends nearby, attending a meeting, at work or, of course, at mushairas and seminars. This was a small silver case, shaped like a book and similar to a cigarette case. It had a decorative top that opened at its hinges to reveal a space that was enough to carry two or three paans, painstakingly made by hand by Amma and wrapped in a damp muslin cloth to prevent them from drying out. Accompanying this case was a little pouch with drawstrings, called a *batua*. This was invariably made by Amma with scraps of brocade, satin or silk. Amma looped a bead at either end of the strings, usually skeins of sturdy red thread, rolled together. This pouch carried two glass bottles, or phials, (washed and repurposed bottles of eye drops, probably prescribed at Gandhi Eye Hospital at some point time) full of tambakhoo, or tobacco powder, and chhaliya. For formal events and soirees, I remember Amma using a beautiful silver butterfly-shaped ornament for serving paan. From the edges of the wings of this palm-sized, intricately filigree-worked butterfly hung segments of delicate silver chains, each with a tiny silver spike or rod at the end. The paans would be threaded through each of the rods and offered to the guests, holding the butterfly. The guest would then help themselves to a paan by gently removing it and putting it in their mouth. It was a delightfully genteel and quaint way to offer paan to esteemed guests. As a child, I longed to adorn my hair with that butterfly, positioning it like a hair clip or *jhoomar*! Of course, I was not allowed to.

A deliciously witty sher with its humorous play on words incorporates both of Abba's beloved things:

Chha liya gham ne terey warna to main aisa kattha
Mushkilein lakh aayein par main choon na kiya

(Your sorrow surrounded me, as I was not like this
Despite all my problems, I never uttered a word)

On a cold winter night, we had a warming meal of arhar ki dal, mooli ki bhujia and rotis for dinner. The arhar ki dal was simply cooked and had a *baghaar* (tempering) of finely sliced garlic in ghee. Someone had visited from Agra that morning and had brought a box of pethey ki mithai. This is passed around. Abba always likes to end his meals with a sweet morsel, or *munh saaf karna*, as he calls it. Nothing elaborate, overly fussy or in a large quantity; just a small bowl of some home-made halwa, a small piece of leftover mithai or a few slices of apple, guava or other seasonal fruit. There is always a little bit of something sweet kept in tins or jars in the old *nematkhana* in the dining room. One of us is asked to fetch it for Abba, which we readily do, helping ourselves to a tasty tidbit en route! Some sweet biscuits, besan laddoos, gurh parey, gazak or something similar. He enjoys his meals and his small sweet indulgences at the end of each meal. Today, of course, he is delighted with his beloved kali gajar ka halwa. He has a small bowl of it and sings its praises. *Kala laya re, kali gajar ka halwa*, he hums with a smile and with closed eyes. He beams at no one in particular and announces, 'Thank you for your kind hospitality', in English, and makes his way to where his books are to immerse himself completely in the world of books . . .

Kali Gajar ka Halwa

1 kg purple carrots, washed, peeled and grated
1 litre full fat milk
1½ cup sugar
2 tbsp asli ghee
3 green cardamom seeds, crushed
½ cup raisins and chopped nuts
½ cup khoya, crumbled

In a large, heavy-bottomed pot, bring the milk to a boil and carefully add the grated carrots. Keep stirring while it cooks on low heat, until most of the milk is evaporated.

Add the ghee, sugar, cardamom powder and most of the chopped nuts, and raisins, saving some for later.

Cook further for a few minutes until glossy.

Once fully halwa-like in consistency, place in a donga or serving dish and crumble the khoya on top, along with the nuts and raisins.

Best enjoyed warm.

~

Abba's lasting legacy to the world of Urdu is his immense and impressive body of work, the numerous books he wrote, such as *Khwab Baqi Hai*, *Nazar Aur Nazariya* and numerous ones on the poet Iqbal, and the establishment of the Iqbal Institute in Srinagar, Kashmir.

Abba greatly influences our lives. We owe our love for Urdu poetry, literature and books in general to him. Recipient of the Sahitya Academy Award in Urdu (1974) and the Padma Bhushan (1992), just to name a few, he always inspires us to strive for greater knowledge and achievements.

> *Sahil ke sukoon se kisey inkar hai lekin*
> *Toofan se larhne mein maza aur hi kuchh*

—Suroor

(The contentment of staying on the riverbank cannot be denied
But the joy of grappling with a storm is something else)

Mummy's Special Shami Kebab

It is the holy month of fasting, Ramzan. Mummy's cousins are visiting, and by a stroke of luck, all of them are in town for a few days. Even Azra Khala has come from Canada, and the air is abuzz with excitement and laughter. Even though all the cousins are married and have children, they reminisce about old times and giggle like schoolgirls. Like the time Nasho Khala donned a borrowed burqa to play a prank on a male relative, pretending to be an ardent admirer and collapsing with laughter halfway through his ordeal and embarrassment. And another time when they were discussing the marital prospects of a boy in the family in the company of elders, tais, chachis, phuppos and dadis (the sisters of Dadi would be addressed as Chhoti Dadi, Majhli Dadi and so on). One of the ladies present was slightly hard of hearing. On being told, '*Ladka adeeb kaamil ho gaya hai* (The boy has gained a graduate degree in Urdu language, *Adeeb-e-Kaamil*, equivalent to a BA degree, from Jamia Urdu Aligarh)', she heard it as '*Ladka ajeeb kaahil ho gaya hai*' (the boy has become strangely lazy)'. She remarked, '*Shadi ke baad achhey achhey sudhar jaatey hain*', causing much mirth and laughter. We sit and listen with awe and amazement as sweet memories from their own youth are retold without rancour or malice. They were a close-knit bunch, with homes close by and roughly similar in ages.

My younger sister wants to keep her very first fast, the *roza*. It involves not eating or drinking anything at all, not even water, from the time of *sehri*, before daybreak, up until *iftar* or sunset. The heat is oppressive, and the hours are long. As she is adamant and wants to progress from the half-day roza she was allowed the previous year, the elders relent and decide to celebrate her very first roza with a special ceremony, the Roza Kushai. The whole family is here to support and celebrate this achievement, and preparations get underway for the function the next day. We are all up at sehri together, eating, drinking copious amounts of water, juice or sherbat and hurriedly filling up on sustenance for the day ahead. My sister gets an alu ka paratha, milk and a few slices of mango to fill her up nicely for the day of fasting ahead.

As it is an important rite of passage and a milestone for a young Muslim child, mummy wants to make something special for the little *rozedar* to mark the occasion. Mummy is Bitto to her own family and is much loved by all her cousins. Soon there will be excited chatter about the feast that will be made to mark the occasion. The cousins have many suggestions, each wanting to make their trademark specialty and bless my sister. The elders call her simply Bitto. Those younger to her call her Bitto Baji, Apa, Khala, Phupi, depending on their link to her in the family tree. Nasho Khala calls her Bhinno—a derivative of behen or sister.

During the day, we are all lazing together on and around the chowki. Amma has large *khus* panels hung like curtains along the outer edge of the veranda. These curtains are made of a kind of dried grass, which, when moistened, not only cools the surrounding air but also perfumes it with the heady, earthy smell of khus. The dense, woven-straw curtains are periodically soaked with water from the hand pump. Out on the veranda, there are also large pedestal fans that rotate noisily. The din of the conversation and the sounds of laughter effectively trounce any disruption by man or machine. The assembled group consists of women of all ages, bound only by a common familial link, mummy. Mummy is a gracious, selfless and caring person who is always the peacemaker in situations such as these, where a stray remark or taunt can easily escalate into warfare and a cold silence stretching over years. Some are more outspoken and sharp-tongued than others, but most prefer to let petty things go during a *mubarak mahina* or month of piety and goodness. Most of us are fasting, and the few who are not, for whatever reason, discreetly go away to eat, away from the fasting ones, out of courtesy or *ehtram*. The afternoon stretches ahead, long and dreary, with our mouths becoming increasingly parched and our energy levels plummeting.

Talk turns to mangoes. It's mango season, and Amma's home is heaving with the sweet aroma of mangoes. Najma Khala has brought a large *peti* (wooden crate) of mangoes from her orchard. Some are in a metal bucket filled with cool water. Others that are not yet ripe are carefully wrapped in old newspapers and kept in a *taaq* to be enjoyed later. This method of ripening fruit is called *paal lagana*. Mangoes are something we are all obsessed with at the moment. We all have our favourites in terms of variety and love our individual choices of mangoes with fervour and ferocity. Abba loves the fragrant and classic yellow, smooth-skinned Dussehri; Amma is partial to a Chausa (late-arriving, intensely vibrant fleshed); Mummy likes Rataul (small but sensationally delicious and sweet); and I absolutely adore Langda (this mango has a little protuberance to a side and its flesh is not at all fibrous). I love its slightly tart but sweet flavour and firm texture. The various other aunts animatedly discuss the pros and cons of different mangoes, and there are mango-related anecdotes and *qisse* (stories) being narrated.

Abba used to tell us about the poet Ghalib's legendary fondness for mangoes and loved to relate this anecdote. A friend of Ghalib who did not care much for mangoes pointed to a donkey standing near a garbage pile of mangoes. And to illustrate the unworthiness of mangoes, he said: '*Dekhiye sahib, gadha tak aam nahi khata*' (Even the donkey doesn't eat mangoes). To which Ghalib, in his customary witty manner, replied, '*Ji, sahi kaha aapne, gadhe aam nahi khate* (Donkeys do not eat mangoes), turning the observation completely on its head. In Urdu usage, a donkey is synonymous with imbecility and a lack of intelligence. It is a delightful anecdote that never fails to make us smile. Another witty comment by Ghalib: when asked about the *khoobiyan* (good qualities) of mangoes, seeing as he was a connoisseur, he replied: '*Aamo mein buss do khoobiyan honi chahiye, ek meethe ho aur bohut saare ho.*'

(In my opinion, there are only two necessary requirements concerning mangoes. They should be sweet and they should be plentiful!)

Abba talks about the many varieties of mangoes mentioned by Ghalib in his letters, which we have never heard of, let alone tasted. These have whimsical, exotic names evocative of bygone times, such as Nazuk Pasand, Fazli Samar Bahisht, Baraah Masi and Rehmat-e-khas. We have tasted the delightfully named Totapari, brought by a visiting friend of Abba and, of course, the famous Alphonso mangoes from Bombay.

The Sufi poet Amir Khusro was enamoured with mangoes too and referred to them as *fakhr-e-gulshan* (pride of the garden).

A witty riddle by Khusro about this glorious fruit is:

Baras baras wo des mein aave
Moonh se monnh laga ras piyave
Va khatir mein kharche daam
Ai sakhi saajan na sakhi aam

(He comes to me every year
He feeds me nectar from his mouth, like kisses
I spend all my money on his welcome
Who is it O friend, your lover?
No, it's a mango)

I find Dussehri too squishy and too orange, and the smell is overpowering. I will happily have it in a mango milkshake, but I am not too keen on eating it whole. On non-fasting days, Mummy cuts off the plump cheek of an unpeeled Langda mango for me and, with a knife, makes a criss-cross pattern on it and pushes up the segments so that little cubes of mango, still attached to the skin underneath, emerge proudly. It looks like a beautiful crown, and I happily eat a few. I have fondness for the *guthli* (the hard stone within, covered with a fibrous layer) too. This is how I always ate mangoes as a child, and many years later, how my children will. Of course, I will always happily spend hours sucking the guthli, extracting the very last bit of the delicious flesh, till it is smooth and ivory-coloured. That simple activity still magically transports me to my childhood.

Soon, the preparations will begin for the evening feast. For the iftar, a traditional and light array of snacks is planned. Dates are customarily used for breaking the fast, or iftar. Detailed accounts of the Prophet (PBUH)'s life indicate that it was his preference to do so too. For this reason, Muslims across the globe follow this practice. It is considered a very blessed fruit and is also very nutritious. Apart from the vitally important dates, there will be dahi badey, shami kebab, miniature qeema-filled samosas and, of course, a lot of sliced mango. There is a piquant and zingy harey dhaniye ki chutney made with bunches of fresh coriander leaves, green chillies and lemon to accompany the kebabs. As Mummy's shami kebabs are legendary, she has offered to make them. Shami kebabs are round, flat, shallow-fried minced-mutton patties made with chaney ki dal, ginger, garlic onions and selected spices. There is Rooh Afza to drink, as well as home-made lemonade.

Shami kebabs, as legend goes, were created to cater to the voracious appetite of a toothless nawab, and so they are soft and smooth in texture. Minced mutton is cooked with onion, ginger, garlic, pre-soaked chaney ki dal and whole spices. Once cooked completely, it is cooled and mashed to a smooth paste. Earlier, it would have been done by hand on a stone slab, but these days most people use a trusty electric blender. These are then shaped into small patties, either plain or stuffed with finely chopped onions, green chillies and fresh coriander leaves for an added enhancement of taste and fragrance. These kebabs are a regular feature at most homes we frequently visit and are made often at our home too. When people are ready to eat, these are shallow-fried and placed on a platter, usually with rings of raw onions and a sprinkle of dhania (coriander) leaves. Some cooks like to dip each kebab in a bowl of beaten egg prior to frying them, but we tend not to do this.

On the subject of kebabs, how can I not mention another idiom that Amma frequently used? 'Cheenti bharey kebab', literally meaning kebabs filled with live ants. This expression was usually used by Amma to describe someone or a situation that looked very tempting, superior or meritorious but was in fact riddled with flaws, unsavoury traits and aspects. This could apply to a *rishta*, or marriage proposal, for a member of the extended family in which the prospective groom seemed like a good catch but Amma knew of some dishonourable, hidden facts about the family. It could also apply to the purchase of a property that had hidden flaws or to something else of value. I am happy to state that the kebabs we ate on this occasion and countless others did not have a trace of ants or other creepy crawlies, for that matter!

Roza Kushai itself is a family affair. Our aunts, uncles and cousins are in attendance. My sister is wearing a new outfit, a pale pink cotton salwar qameez that Naseem Khala embroidered with beautiful rosebuds. She is wearing a hand-dyed pink and white wavy-patterned, or *lehriya chunna*, dupatta that has been painstakingly hand-crinkled along the length by Ruqayya Khala and Nasho Khala. The process of crinkling is a delicate one, using the *kalaf (maarh)*, or starch, from boiling rice and, when cooled, rubbing the dupatta back and forth along its length with starch-dipped finger tips. Each crinkle or *chunnat* is painstakingly produced by a skillful pill-rolling movement, working through various sections.

The dupatta is always a plain white mulmul cotton one, to start with. A *dhanak*, or rainbow-coloured stripes or patterns are made using little bowls of different coloured dyes. The names of the colours are pure poetry:

surkh (red)
gulabi (pink)
pyazi (pale pink)
narangi (orange)

sabz or *kaahi* (green)

dhaani (pale green)

aasmani (light blue)

zard (yellow)

kishmishi, badami (light brown)

katthai (hazel brown)

faqtai (beige)

firozi (turquoise)

siyah (black)

ooda or *baingani* (deep purple)

salaytee (grey)

unnabi (intense purple)

phalsaee (mauve)

banafshi (violet)

kasni (lavender, shade of purple)

sunehra (golden)

rupehla (silvery)

rani rang (deep magenta)

arghwani (deep reddish brown)

zaafraani (saffron coloured)

Of course, these beautiful, evocative words often find themselves mentioned in Urdu poetry.

For instance,

> **Surkh** *aahan par tapakti boond hai ab har khushi*
> *Zindagi ne yun toh pehle ham ko tarsaya na tha*

—Qateel Shifai

(Each happiness of mine drops to sizzle on a red-hot iron
Life never mocked me thus)

*. . . **Zard** patton ka ban jo mera des hai*
Dard ki anjuman jo mera des hai . . .

—Faiz Ahmad Faiz

(The forest of yellowed leaves that is my land
The collective of pain that is my land)

*Neend ka halka **gulabi** sa khumar ankhon mein tha*
Yun laga jaise vo shab ko der tak soya nahi

—Muneer Niyazi

(Sleep gave his eyes a pale pink drowsiness
It seemed that he did not sleep till late in the night)

*Dekh kar kurtey halkey mein sabz **dhaani** aap ki*
dhaan ke bhi khet ne ab aan maani aap ki

—Nazeer Akbarabadi

(Looking at the green embroidery at the neck of your shirt
The fields of paddy too are impressed by your appearance)

The word **katthai** was popularized in the late 1990s by poet and lyricist Javed Akhtar in a song from the film *Duplicate*.

***Katthai** ankhon wali ek ladki*
ek hi baat par bigarhti hai . . .

(The hazel-eyed girl
gets upset by just one thing)

Kishwar Naheed, too, uses this word skillfully:

> **Katthai** rang ghule surmai shaam mein aise ki shafaq
> Khoon ki aanchon se dahak kar phaile

(The deep brown merges with the dark skies of the evening
It is as if the twilight colours have blazed together with blood)

> Rang gardun ka zara dekh toh **unnabi** hai
> Ye nikalte hue suraj ki ufaq-tabi hai

—Allama Iqbal

(Oh, just look at the purple of the sky
It is the brilliance of the rising sun)

Faiz mentions the colour **kaasni** in his legendary nazm, '*Tum mere paas raho*', immortalized by the wonderful Nayyara Noor, thus:

> . . . Bain karti hui hasti hui gaati nikley
> Dard ke **kaasni** paazeb bajati nikley

(The dark night passes, lamenting, laughing and singing
Jangling the purple anklets of pain)

Sunehra finds itself in many poetic compositions, with gold or golden being not just a metaphor for all that is auspicious or precious but also for purity and brilliance.

> Har-chand nazar ne jhele hain har bar **sunehre** ghaav bhi
> Hum aaj bhi dhoka kha lengey tum bhes badal kar aao bhi

—Qateel Shifai

(Although I have endured glorious wounds
I can still be fooled, even if you come in in a different guise)

Rupehla, the silvery sheen, finds its way in these delightful lines:

Wahi pyare madhur alfaz mithi ras bhari baatein
*wahi raushan **rupehle** din vahi mahki hui ratein*
—Khalil-ur-Rahman Azmi

(Those lovely, melodious words, those sweet conversations
Those bright, silvery days, those fragrant nights)

The colours of dupattas are just as manifold as the colours of *choorhiyan*, or glass bangles, and are beautifully expressed:

Apna apna rang dikhlati hain jaani choorhiyan
aasmani, arghwani zaafrani choorhiyan
—Syed Yusuf Ali Khan Nazim

(The glass bangles display their varied colours
sky blue, puce, saffron bangles)

The dupattas themselves are just as lyrical, special and beautiful. Nasho Khala loves to make a *chand aur sooraj* design (crescent moon and sun), using the rim of a bowl. Sometimes, a simple *doriya*, or string, is tied tightly along the length at regular intervals, forming colour blocks of white and coloured patterns along the length, similar to a tie-dye technique. It looks like a coiled serpent when wound up into a loose ball to dry the starch and keep the crinkles intact. The crinkled dupatta, when worn, unfurls ever so slightly like a concertina and elegantly swings from the shoulders, draping yet retaining its shape, bedecking the neck and skimming the upper torso. There is a faint glimmer along the dupatta due to a fine sprinkling of *abrak* or glitter. My sister leaves behind a trail of sparkly dust as the flecks are shed gently, like leaves from a tree in autumn. She is wearing bright pink and green glass bangles, specially bought for her from Ferozabad. They have flecks of gold embossed on the smooth glass and look very special. The various kinds of bangles themselves have quaint, sweet names. The dhaani chooriyan for the pale-green ones, also called *kareliyan*, worn by young girls in *saawan* (monoon) season; the zig-zag ones called *bankey*; the golden hollow ones, favoured by Nasho Khala, called *phoonkiyan*; and the scarlet bangles that *suhagans* (married women) wear with pride.

My sister gets small presents like a dupatta or small silver *jhumke* (earrings) or money in hand-stitched batue and everyone blesses her. Everyone is proud of her for successfully completing her first roza.

Special preparations have been made to make the heat a bit more bearable. Before the arrival of others, a *chhirhkao*, or dousing, of the concrete courtyard is done using buckets of water to cool the surface and also evoke the earthy sensation of petrichor. A few pedestal fans are strategically placed to provide some much-needed cool air. Hunger and thirst make the heat even more oppressive, and we all try to keep ourselves busy and calm. This month is not just about fasting but also good deeds, piety and kindness.

After the iftar, there is a gap for the evening prayers, followed by dinner. We are having biryani made by Naseem Khala, lauki ka raita and a chicken qorma cooked by Najma Khala. It's a never-ending feast, as very soon we will be up for the pre-dawn meal of sehri for the next day's fast.

The conversations and nostalgic reminiscing carry on for a while longer after namaz has been offered. We youngsters listen with fascination to stories about older relatives, some of whom we never got to meet. Like a witty Chhoti Dadi who coined the phrase we still use in our family to this date, when exasperated with the antics of our children: *'Bahiniya bache barhi mushkil se paltey hain'* (Sister, it is difficult to raise children). It lends a feeling of sisterhood, like 'We've all been there' or 'I totally get what you are feeling'.

Shami Kebab

½ kg minced mutton or your choice of minced meat
½ cup chana dal, washed and soaked for 1 hour
1 cinnamon stick, 2–3 inches long
2 black cardamoms
1 medium to large onion, chopped
3 cloves of garlic
½ tsp ginger paste
4–5 whole cloves
1 dried red chilli, broken up in pieces
salt to taste

For the stuffing (optional):
1–2 green chillies, finely chopped
fresh coriander leaves, finely chopped
red onion, finely chopped
2 tbsp oil to fry

Place the soaked, drained chana dal, minced meat and everything except the ingredients for stuffing and oil in a heavy-bottomed, lidded pot.

Cook for about 30–35 minutes on low heat until the chana dal is cooked and tender. With a large wooden spoon, mix well and bring everything together. Pick out and discard the cloves, cinnamon sticks and cardamom if you prefer. The mixture should be fairly dry and lumpy. Use a hand blender or traditional mixer to turn this into a smooth, beige-coloured putty-like consistency.

Chill in the refrigerator until you are ready to fry the kebabs.

Make plum-sized balls, slightly flatten and place ½-tsp-sized onion mixture for the filling. Skip the filling if you are making ahead to freeze.

Flatten into patties and shallow fry them in a frying pan. Treat them gently, as they are delicate. Brown them nicely on either side.

~

Other commonly made dishes for iftar are as follows:

When kamrakh, also known as star fruit, this bright chartreuse-coloured fruit with its deep ridges down its sides, is in season, we greatly enjoy it. It is a popular snack for us as children. Simply slitting with a sharp knife with a spicy rock salt and chilli-laden masala was enough to send us in raptures. It is intensely tart; there is no getting around it. The first bite into it, spraying droplets of its sour, sharp juice mixed with the piquant masala smells in the air, could make you wince. But like any other childhood treat, it only goaded us to eat more of it. It is called star fruit in English because, when cut crosswise, the sections look like stars.

There is a kamrakh tree that grows at the home of a distant family member. We often get sent baskets of their bounty. I often snatch a few before a zingy chutney is made from them, deaf to the admonishing voices of elders warning about dire consequences, including getting a sore throat!

Kamrakh ki Chutney

2 kamrakh, washed
a small bunch of fresh coriander leaves, washed
2–3 fresh green chillies, depending on your preference
a few sprigs of fresh mint leaves, stems discarded
salt to taste
roasted and powdered cumin seeds.

Peel and deseed the kamrakh and cut into chunks.
 Blend everything into a fine paste. Check seasoning, and serve.
 This chutney is great with very meaty dishes, as the sourness cuts through the unctuousness of meat and makes it even more flavoursome and fresh tasting for the palate.
 Another refreshing and healthy dish served on most days during Ramzan was this fruit-based concoction called kachalu. We always associate pungent smells and bursts of flavour and texture with iftar times.

Kachalu

2–3 ripe bananas
2 apples
2 oranges
a bunch of grapes, preferably seedless
1–2 chikoo
1–2 ripe guavas
1 tsp sugar, optional
¼ tsp rock salt
½ tsp freshly ground pepper
juice of 1 lemon
½ tsp red chilli powder
¼ tsp roasted cumin powder
10–15 pomegranate seeds

You can skip or substitute any fruit as long as it is juicy and can be cut into chunks.

In a large serving bowl, peel and chop the bananas into roundels. Chop the apples and guavas into small chunks. Peel the chikoo and chop into chunks.

Remove the grapes from their stems and wash thoroughly. Peel and take out the segments of oranges, removing any seeds and pith.

Add them all to the bowl.

Add sugar, salt, red chilli powder, rock salt, pepper, roasted cumin powder and lemon juice, and gently mix. Cover with a plate for about 20 minutes before it is ready to be eaten.

You can also scatter a few pomegranate seeds on top for a burst of jewel-like colour and to add texture and flavour.

Ubley Kaaley Chaney

This nutritious, protein-packed dish strangely makes its way only in the month of Ramzan in most homes—ours most certainly. The tiny dark brown chana, or brown chickpeas, are soaked overnight so they are softer and easier to cook with.

2 cups kala chana, soaked overnight
1 tsp cumin seeds
1 onion, finely chopped
1 tsp coriander powder
1 tsp red chilli powder
½ tsp turmeric powder
salt to taste
1 bay leaf
1 tbsp cooking oil

½ tsp amchur (dried mango powder)
a bunch of washed fresh coriander leaves
juice of a lemon and a few wedges of lemon
1 or 2 fresh green chillies, depending on your preference
chaat masala, optional

Boil the soaked chana and simmer until cooked.

In a karhai, add the oil and when hot, add the onions, bay leaf and spices. Saute this for a few minutes and then add the channey, stirring them through.

Check the seasoning. Add amchur and chopped fresh coriander for garnish.

Can be served hot or cold.

~

Food is an integral part of all family get-togethers, even funerals. At these, qorma, tandoori roti from a local tandoor and seekh kebab are the standard fare. Meals are eaten, people stay on for a while, reminiscing about the one who has departed, and then head home. Life goes on as before, with the circle of life ensuring newer additions to the family, either by birth or through marriage.

While on the topic of kebab, one cannot resist reciting this delightful sher by the poet Ameer Meenai, albeit for a different kind of kebab:

Kebab-e-seekh hain hum karvatein har soo badaltey hain
Jal utha jo yeh pehlu to wo pehlu badaltey hain

(I am akin to a seekh (skewered) kebab, turning continuously
When one side starts to burn, I change my position)

Naseem Khala's Extraordinary Firni

We are visiting Amma for our school holidays. I have cleared my Class X board exams and, for a while, have been free of any care or vexatious issues. Amma has decided to host a *meelad*. A meelad is a religious gathering in which praises of the Prophet (PBUH) are sung and recited and is a celebration of his birth and life. The event is known as *Eid-e-Meelad-un-Nabi*. The day falls on the 12th of Rabi-ul-Awwal, the third month of the Muslim lunar calendar, so it varies from year to year in the Western calendar. Amma usually does a ladies-only meelad in which women from the extended family, friends and neighbours are invited. It takes place in the afternoon, around tea-time, and is followed by an elaborate tea set out for the attendees. It is not a very formal gathering, but as there are about fifty to sixty women expected, it is an operation that needs almost military-style planning and execution. We all have our assigned roles and jobs, both in the days prior to the event and on the day itself.

The veranda is where the meelad will be held. The chowki is moved out into the courtyard, though a section of it will be brought in later and placed at one end of the veranda to seat the ladies who will be reciting and singing. There are no musical instruments, as it is a solemn gathering. The floor is cleaned, swept and washed by the cleaner. Once it's dry, a large durrie is spread out on it. It is one of the usual geometric designs, with a blue-grey section merging into a section of dull pink, that are commonly seen at weddings and other outdoor functions. At least two of these massive durries are needed to cover the floor space. On the day of the meelad, a pure white dhobi-washed and ironed sheet will be spread over the durrie. We youngsters are forbidden from walking over the sheets with our grubby shoes or sullying them in any way! Amma refers to these pristine sheets as *chandni*, which conjures up images of milky-white moonlight bathing dark corners in its silvery light. Some colourful *gao takiyas*, or large elongated bolster cushions, covered in a dark velvety material, are placed at strategic locations on the chandni. These are for the comfort of the seated ladies, as a form of back support, and also make the seating area look welcoming. A few rose blooms, plucked from the rose bush in the courtyard, are arranged in a beautiful and elegant antique silver vase, and the air is redolent with their heady fragrance. Pedestal fans to bring some relief in the hot weather are placed alongside the seating area.

On the small raised platform, or chowki, will be another thin mattress and a chandni, along with more gao takiyas and cushions in beautiful embroidered silk covers. The ladies who will recite are relatives or neighbours. Each has her own chosen contribution. First, a recitation of a few chosen verses from the holy Quran takes place. Then one of the readers recites verses describing the conditions of the Prophet's birth and of life in Arabia at the time. Others will sing a few soulful *naat*, or hymns, in praise of the Prophet. His qualities as a person are extolled, as are his kind and modest actions. His wisdom and strength of character are other themes that are essential features of these verses. The words are highly emotive, evoking love, respect and admiration for the Prophet. The compilation of these naat and *hamd* is in Amma's copy of the much-loved and revered book of *Meelad-e-Akbar*.

The beginning of the meelad is heralded with a few lines that originate in the book.

> *Darbar-e-aam garm hua, ishtahar do*
> *Jinn-o-bashar salaam ko aayein, pukar do*
> *Kar do khabar yeh mehfil-e-shah hai*
> *Ummat chaley rasool ki yeh jalwa gah hai*

> (The public hall welcomes you warmly
> All are welcome, call for them to congregate respectfully
> Tell them that it is a majestic gathering
> We are the followers of the Prophet
> This is a place of splendour and piety)

A hamd praising Allah is usually recited at the beginning of the meelad. In Amma's home it could be:

> *Tujhe dhoondhta tha main char su, teri shaan jall-e-jalal hu*
> *Tu mila qareeb rag-e-gulu, teri shaan jall-e-jalal hu*

> (I looked for you everywhere; your grace is the most glorious of all
> You are always in our midst; your grace is the most glorious of all)

A naat singing the praises of the Prophet usually follow:

> *Har dard ki dawa hai Salle-Ala Muhammad*
> *Taweez har bala hai Salle-Ala Muhammad*
> *Mehboobe-e-kibriya hai Salle-Ala Muhammad*
> *Kya naqsh khushnuma hai Salle-Ala Muhammad*

> (He is the cure for all the pains and troubles
> He is the remedy for all misfortune
> He has glory and grandeur
> His persona is most pleasant)

Another naat describes his kindness, helping the needy and poor, a saviour of those in grief and difficult times:

> *Woh Nabiyon mein rehmat laqab paaney wala*
> *Muradein Gharibon ki bar laney wala*
> *Museebat mein ghairon kay kaam aaney wala*
> *Woh apney paraye ka gham khaney wala*

> (He is the greatest of the prophets
> He fulfils the aspirations of the poor and needy
> He looks after the forgotten
> He takes away your sorrows)

A soulful naat describing one's yearning and desperation to visit the holy mosque at Madina, a symbol of piety and faith:

> *Faaslon ko takalluf hai humse agar*
> *Hum bhi bebas nahi besahara nahi*

Khud unhi ko pukarenge hum door se
Rastey mein agar paon thak jayenge
Hum Madiney mein tanha nikal jayenge
Aur galiyon mein kuch din bhatak jayenge

(The journey may be long and arduous
But I am determined and not devoid of hope
I will call out for his support and assurance
If I were to get tired on the way
I will visit Madina by myself
And lose myself in the streets for a few days)

Another naat that expresses a true believer's longing for a pilgrimage to the holy city of Madina or describing his intense emotions while undertaking the holy pilgrimage:

Madine ka safar hai aur main namdeda namdeda
Jabeen afsurda afsurda qadam laghzeeda laghzeeda
Chala hoon ek mujrim ki tarha main janib e taiba
Nazar sharminda sharminda badan larzeda larzeda
Kisi ke hath ney mujh ko sahara dey diya warna
Kahan mey aur kahan ye rasta pechida pechida

(On my way to Madina, my eyes well up with tears
I am pensive, unsteady on my feet
I am remorseful, thinking of my sins and feel nervous
Someone gave me support when I needed it, as I made this
arduous journey)

Taazeem se leta hai Khuda naam-e-Muhammad
Kya naam hai ai salle ala nam e . . .

Quran mein Jannat mein sar-e-arsh sar-e-lau
Kis shaan se Khaaliq ne likha naam-e-Muhammad

(His name is taken with utmost respect
His fame and glory is boundless
In the Quran, in heaven, in the sky and on the Earth,
The Creator has written his name with pride everywhere)

Some naat celebrating his *paidaish*, or birth:

Aae Muhammad Mustafa
Ehlan wa sehlan marhaba
Salle ala salle ala
Ehlan wa sehlan marhaba
Makke mein phaili roshni
Yesrib mein chitki chandni
Paida huey badruduja,
Ehlan wa sehlan marhaba

(We welcome the birth of the holy Prophet (PBUH) and
rejoice in it
Glory be to him
We rejoice in his birth
There is light over the city of Mecca, and over Madinah
The one who brings brightness over the dark night
The Prophet (PBUH) is born)

This naat is very special to me as it was the first one that I learned
from a dear family friend, Najma aunty, a very talented and erudite
lady who was a professor in the English department at AMU. We
practised it several times together and then I recited it in the actual
meelad alongside her. It is a testament to her patience that I can
still recite this even today, entirely from memory.

Another sweet, melodious naat uses a garden as metaphor for humanity and describes the arrival of the Prophet (PBUH) and the resultant flourishing and vitality in the garden:

> *Aamad e Mustafa se hai, phoola phala chaman chaman*
> *Aayi bahaar har taraf khilne laga chaman chaman*
> *Thhandi hawayein aati hain, kaliyan bhi muskurati hain*
> *Bulbulein cheh chahati hain khilne laga chaman chaman*

> (With the arrival of the Prophet (PBUH), the garden is vibrant
> There is rejoicing and there are flowers in full bloom
> Cool breeze flows and the buds seem to smile
> The birds are chirping and the garden prospers)

In between the recitations, the listeners are asked to read the holy verse of Durood sharif to themselves:

> *Durood parho, aashiqon Durood parho*

> (Read the Durood, those who love the Almighty)

Reading the Durood sharif is a means of obtaining the mercy of Allah and purifying one's heart and mind.

Towards the end of the meelad, we all stand up and join in reciting the salaam, to honour His greatness:

> *Ya nabi salam alaika, ya rasool salam alaika*
> *Ya habeeb salam alaika sala wa tulla alaika*
> *Jaan ke kafi sahara*
> *Le liya hai dar tumhara*

Khalq ke waris khudara
Lo salam ab to hamara

(We greet you with respect, O Holy Prophet (PBUH)
We come to you for support and your munificence
O saviour of mankind
Accept our humble greetings)

Another well-known salaam is:

Mustafa jaan e rehmat pe lakhon salaam
Shama e bazam e hidayat pe lakhon salaam

(Greetings O benevolent Prophet (PBUH)
We greet you with respect, our guiding light)

Dua is read at the very end of the meelad:

Momino waqt-e rehmat-e rab hai
Ab wo maango jo dil ka maqsad hai
Sabko rabb e Ghafoor deta hai
Hai who data zaroor deta hai

(Believers, it is the time of benevolence by the Almighty
Ask for what your heart seeks
He is full of kindness
He gives with generosity)

My sister and I have been given the task of going to each of
the attendees to daub a little *itr*, or perfume, from an *itrdani*

on their wrists. It is an important ritual. We solemnly make
our way, kneeling on the chandni and moving adroitly on our
knees, heads bowed, carrying out the task assigned to us. There
is already a heady fragrance in the air from sandalwood *agarbattis*
(incense sticks) and fresh rose petals. The itr is musky and sweet-
smelling. The itrdani is a beautiful silver filigreed container with
a tight-fitting domed cap that we must replace carefully after use;
otherwise, the magical perfume, reminiscent of jasmines in full
bloom on a summer's night, with notes of kewra (pandanus) and
khus, will dissipate.

The atmosphere is one of piety and blessedness. All those
present in the meelad raise their palms in front and in their
minds, ask for their dearest and most personal wishes to be
granted. *Ameen*, so be it, is said afterwards.

The meelad has come to an end. The ladies get up and
murmur appreciatively at the choice of verses and naat, and it
becomes a social gathering with women embracing one another
and greeting old acquaintances and friends. Behind the scenes,
there has been frenetic activity in the kitchen, with large
quantities of tea being prepared and then poured into fine china
tea cups. These are then placed on large trays and carried to
where the ladies are gathered. Along with steaming cups of tea,
there is fresh, salty namak para and hot samosas from the local
halwai (sweet seller), and a very special item of food.

Naseem Khala, who is visiting from Badayun, is the eldest
of the cousins and shares a very close bond with Amma. Amma
makes no distinction in her affections for her own daughter and
her, and she, in turn, looks up to Amma and seeks her advice
regarding clothes, jewellery and other household matters. She is
the daughter of Abba's older brother, our mother's Tau. Naseem
Khala is a strikingly handsome woman with sharp, chiselled

features who wears a twinkling diamond nose stud. She has jet-black, very curly hair tied into a thick braid that reaches her waist. She has a brisk, no-nonsense air about her and dresses very practically and austerely. Today she is wearing what she calls a *kishmishi* (sort of brown, raisin-coloured) cotton sari. She has tucked her *pallu* into her sari waistband as she busies herself, overseeing everything in the kitchen and making sure everything is perfectly organized.

Amma affectionately calls her Nassan. Occasionally sharp of tongue and stern, she is nevertheless affectionate and caring. The younger cousins are slightly in awe of her and look to her for advice, approval and help. She herself has a large brood, all much older than us, but still finds the time and energy to come to the aid of anyone needing support in sickness, childbirth or other events. She is the first person to reach if a family member in the clan has passed on, even if it means taking an arduous train journey, and she effortlessly slips into running the household, managing day-to-day tasks and cooking for the family and visitors. She is capable and well-versed in the rituals and religious obligations for all situations. And people automatically defer to her and follow her instructions. She is an accomplished cook and a skilled seamstress, creating elaborately embroidered and artfully stitched outfits with the same ease as conjuring up *deghs* (large pots) of mouth-watering food in minutes, as if by magic. She has had a brilliant idea, one that Amma heartily approves of.

She has prepared a vast degh of firni and then poured it into earthenware bowls, bringing in dozens from the local *kumhar* (potter). The firni is made with milk, ground rice and sugar. It sets when cooled into a firm, pudding-like consistency and looks stunning in the little bowls, garnished with delicate slivers of almonds, a sprinkling of desiccated coconut and a silvery shimmer of *chaandi ke warq*. These bowls are also carried over, along with tiny spoons, and prove to be extremely popular amongst the guests. The earthy aroma from the earthen bowl mingles with the melt-in-the-mouth texture and deliciously creamy and flavoursome taste of the firni to create something that is truly special and delectable. The meelad has been a huge success, and all the hard work that went into it seems worthwhile. Minor slip-ups are overlooked and laughed at. We get better at it with every passing year!

As the guests prepare to leave, another important task remains. Each guest is given a *hissa*, or blessed offering. Each year, Amma decides to distribute balushahi for the hissa. These had been made fresh by the halwai and delivered to her house earlier in the day in a large woven bamboo basket, like the ones used for a fruit basket or hamper. Amma likes to call a basket like this a *jhauaa*. Along with the balushahi, the halwai also sends about sixty small, coloured paper bags. It is our job to carefully and quickly place a set number of balushahi in each bag, tie it up with a small piece of silver *gota* (tinsel ribbon) and place it on a platter. We have to be careful when we handle these, as they are quite fragile and soft. Balushahis are a traditional mithai, round and flaky with sugar syrup soaked within the layers, but unlike gulab jamuns, the syrup is not drippy, so they are a bit easier to handle and place in the little *thailiyan* (bags). They smell delicious, and we fight the temptation to gulp down a few when no one is looking. There is an assembly line of us siblings. One person fills the bags, the other cuts up similar lengths of silver-coloured gota from a large roll and the third ties the gota in a pretty bow to seal the little bags. We are exhausted, and there is still so much to do. Some bags are bright yellow, others are vivid pink and some are lime green. They look beautiful nestling together on the large, engraved Moradabadi brass platter, or *seeni*, slightly tarnished and scratched over the years of constant use, which somehow adds to its charm. A patchy dark patina gives it interesting convoluting patterns and a touch of mystery. We feel justifiably proud of ourselves. It will be our job to hand these bags to each of the guests as they leave.

The guests have all left, and we fondly reminisce and chatter about the day. The men of the household, who had until now been hovering in their rooms, also come out and enjoy the food and conversation. We soon set about clearing up and putting away the items used. It was quite an event! What's even more wonderful is that there is still plenty of Naseem Khala's firni left for us to enjoy later.

Naseem Khala, of course, busies herself with numerous tasks rather than resting on her laurels and is soon going to start planning for a similar meelad at her sister Najma Khala's home in a few days. The social network is a powerful tool, eliminating the need to call outside help. Everyone pitches in, knowing others will do the same for them.

Firni

Chaandi ka warq is a quintessential feature of most Indian mithais and is really the thinnest slivers of silver beaten to form membrane-like delicate sheets within layers of parchment paper to separate them.

(Feeds 10–12)
1 cup ground raw rice
1 litre full-fat milk
1 cup sugar

¾ cup chopped dry fruit, nuts and raisins (mewa*)
1 tbsp desiccated coconut
3–4 ground cardamom seeds
4–5 drops kewra
silver warq, as needed
2 tbsp slivers of peeled almonds and chopped pistachios

Bring the milk to a boil and keep it aside.

First mix the ground rice in a little milk to make a paste, and then add some more milk so there are no lumps.

Add the mixture to a heavy-bottomed pot, and place on heat.

Stir continuously with a spoon over low heat and add the rest of the milk.

Once the mixture thickens somewhat, add the ground cardamom.

Keep stirring continuously to avoid sticking to the bottom of the pan, and keep the heat low.

Now add the sugar and stir to fully mix it in.

Then add the chopped dry fruit and nuts.

Add 4–5 drops of kewra.

Take off the pan and ladle it into washed earthenware bowls.

Sprinkle with slivers of almonds and chopped pistachios.

Decorate with fragments of warq and let it cool.

The earthenware pots are not absolutely necessary, but they add an authentic touch and imbue the firni with a tantalizingly earthy aroma.

---

* The quantity of ingredients like mewa are never exact. If questioned, the home cook would retort, a trifle impatiently, 'Tumhare paas jitni, daal do!' No one weighs or measures these things.

Another dish that Naseem Khala made with great relish and pride was a simple one, but with her *haath ka maza* (special skill), elevated to something sublime and soul-satisfying. It was bringing together two very humble and unremarkable ingredients and creating an alchemy—a confluence of textures, flavours and an unexpected luxurious taste—to rival any meat preparation. Ask anyone who has eaten this with hot rotis, and they will agree, hand on heart.

Lauki Chana Dal

Lauki, or bottle gourd, is a humble vegetable that is considered rather bland and uninteresting by some. However, this pairing with chana dal elevates it to a very special and delectable status. The contrast of textures, colours and flavours, and especially the gloriously ghee-laden *baghaar* (tempering) with friable, delicately browned onions and the fragrance of slit green chillies, is truly magical. The preparation of adhan is also a factor in flavouring the dal, imbuing it with its intense spices.

1 cup chana dal washed, soaked overnight
1 lauki

For the adhan:
1 tsp ginger-garlic paste
1 tsp coriander powder
1 tsp red chilli powder
1 tsp turmeric powder
salt to taste

Make adhan:

Add all the adhan ingredients to 2 cups of water, and bring to a boil in a large pan.

Simmer for a few minutes until the raw smell disappears. Keep aside.

Meanwhile, wash, peel, deseed and chop the lauki into roughly 1-inch sized chunks.

Place the soaked dal, adhan and pieces of lauki in a pressure cooker and cook for 15 minutes.

Carefully transfer to a serving bowl.

To prepare the baghaar:

1 tbsp pure ghee

½ small onion, thinly sliced

In a small frying pan, heat the ghee and add the sliced onion.

Gently fry until crisp and golden brown.

Pour the baghaar over the dal

For the garnish:

a pinch of garam masala

2–3 fresh green chillies

a sprig of fresh coriander leaves, chopped

Sprinkle garam masala and scatter slit fresh green chillies on the lauki dal.

Finish with chopped fresh coriander leaves.

~

Hosting these functions, delegating tasks and, in the process, bringing blessings for the house and for all those who attended was an act not just of piety but also required great organizational skills. We did not learn these at school or, for that matter, later at universities. We imbibed these by observing, getting involved and completely owning them. The elaborate preparations could be tedious and time-consuming, but we felt a huge sense of achievement afterwards. The words spoken at the gathering may have meant little to us at that time; the hymns mouthed without much thought, but they were all ingraining a deep belief in us. It also meant that these rituals would carry on to the next generation. Supplications such as these are a way of involving everyone—family, friends, neighbours and loved ones. We learn the most important lessons in life. Pray to the Almighty, and always be grateful and humble.

> *Yahi hai ibadat yahi din o ima*
> *Ki kaam aaye duniya mein insaan ke insaan*
>
> —Altaf Husain Hali

(This is the act of praying, this is faith and moral principles
that in this world, the inhabitants should help one another)

Ruqqaiyya Khala's Gratifying
Chuqandar Gosht

It is a crisp winter afternoon in Amma's home. The gentle sunlight filters through the trees onto the courtyard, where we youngsters are sprawled on rugs on the brickwork pattern of the courtyard, munching on roasted peanuts and lumps of *gur*, or jaggery. There is a plate with a mound of cracked peanut shells and a confetti-like trail of tiny bits of their red skin that we peel off and blow away. The roasted peanuts have a wonderful, earthy aroma and are freshly roasted by the vendor, who plies his trade from a small, two-wheeled cart just across the road. There are heaps of roasted chana (chickpeas), murmure (puffed rice) and peanuts. He also stocks sweet treats like gud ki patti, known to us Delhiites as chikki (peanut and jaggery brittle) and rewri (small discs made with sesame seeds and jaggery). These quintessential snacks or treats are what make lazy winter afternoons such a joy, and we relish them all. The freshly roasted peanuts are still warm in their paper bags, made from an old copy of a local newspaper. The gur comes from a lala's shop and is of reputedly good quality. Light amber in colour, crumbly and without visible impurities, it comes as a whole large disc, the size of a dinner

plate, known as bheli. People chisel off chunks from it as they
need. When Amma has some free time, she will make several
jars of brittle, but with walnuts, Bournvita and milk powder! It is
a complicated process for which we are all duly recruited. A lot
of pulling and gathering of a warm and sticky mortar-like treacle
substance is involved. The end result is fantastic—fudgier than
the usual brittle type but still with a bite to it. There is a deep
caramel–chocolate flavour to it, which is quite different from
your run-of-the-mill chikki. We love it and eat copious amounts
of it. Of course, when Amma's gur creation eventually finishes,
we happily munch on the usual peanut brittle. The grown-ups,
sitting on wrought-iron outdoor chairs, are engrossed in their
conversations concerning household matters, and we have
absolutely no interest in that. The cushions on those seats have
been hand stitched by Amma, from leftover yard-lengths of
chintzy cloths, with the cotton wool stuffing rescued from old,
limp *razais* (quilts). Therefore, the cushions come in a plethora
of colours and patterns, adding a dash of cheer to the *aangan*
(courtyard). There is a distant *thuk-thuk* sound of a hammer and
the grating sound of a piece of wood being manually sawed. A
handyman is hard at work, working on some broken kitchen
cabinets and faulty doors. He comes highly recommended by
Qaiser Khala, who is not a relative but a family friend. She had
sent the man over as he had earlier done some work at her house.

There are many winter snacks or treats specific to this season
and this region of India. Home-made snacks such as sautéed and
spicy green peas, choker ki puri, gajar ka halwa, shaljam ka achar
and til ke laddoo just to name a few. Not only are these comfort
foods, but they also bring warmth to the body and ultilize the
season's offerings to the fullest. The winter spell, though brief,
can be unduly harsh and body-numbingly cold. Indoors, people

huddle together, women in shawls and many layers of woollens, men in warm jackets and scarves, and children in hand-knitted woolly hats, rubbing their hands together in the vicinity of a small electric heater that glows and casts an amber shadow on all. The few hours of weak sunshine, when it is not foggy, bring respite and we make the most of them.

There isn't much to do in this cold weather, so we have borrowed some books from Abba's extensive library at home. There are countless books, in English and Urdu, on topics as diverse as a garden full of many kinds of flowers. On poetry, literature, history, fiction and biographies, just to name a few. We can always find something to interest us. Abba has written numerous books himself and is very well regarded in the world of academia. I love the dusty, very slightly musty smell of the older books and eagerly try to find something that captures my attention. There are rows upon rows of bookcases from the floor almost to the ceiling, in a room dedicated to them. But the books are so numerous that they spill over to more bookshelves and glass-fronted cabinets, all along the gallery leading to the room and in the dining room. I think Abba instilled in all of us a love of books and poetry and a thirst for knowledge.

Many of the women in the family, including our mother, have received university education and are well read. Amma, though not formally educated beyond school, is a voracious reader of Urdu periodicals and journals. She writes her *hisaab*, or household budgeting, in a small notebook and manages all the finances, be they bank accounts, salaries of servants, petty cash and *raashan*, or groceries. And she still manages to save her pennies to buy a very occasional trinket for herself, a daughter or a niece. When money is tight, she will take an unloved or broken piece of jewellery to her trusty *sunaar*, or jeweller, and have him melt it down or exchange it for a few smaller pieces, a *tola* here, a *masha* there. A sparkly pair of new *jhumkiyan* (earrings) for a girl's graduation, an *angoothi* (ring) for a new bride or a delicate *naak ki keel*, a nose stud, for a young girl passing matric, all from an old, misshapen, broken *kangan* (bracelet) that was part of her own wedding jewellery. When Amma returns triumphantly from a visit to the sunaar, holding precious little boxes and unwraps the deep pink kite paper with precious trinkets nestling within its folds, we are reminded of the famous dialogue in the 1962 Guru Dutt film, *Saheb Bibi Aur Ghulam*: 'Gehne banwao, gehne tudwao . . .', and we dramatically mouth it, just like the imperious, dismissive Rehman's character did. This leads to much mirth, and we excitedly examine the wares. The younger children have to make do with silver jewellery: a *pariband* (charm bracelet) that twinkles on our arms, *bichhue* (toe rings) or chains with a pendant, usually a coloured stone. Proper, grown-up jewellery is, of course, always pure gold, plain or *jadau*, set with vibrantly pink *yaqoot* rubies or leafy green *panna* (emeralds), *moti* (pearls), *heerey* (diamonds) and very rarely other precious gemstones such as *firoza* (turquoise), *pukhraj* (topaz) and *moonga* (coral).

Jewellery worn in the earlobes has evocative, whimsical names—*jhumke, jhaale, baaliyan* and *jhumke karanphool*—with a flower-shaped upper part. Jewellery worn on the wrists includes kangan, *jadau* kangan (encrusted with precious stones) and *paunchiyan*, a bracelet made from black or red velvet on which are studded dozens of bunched little balls of lac covered with a thin plating of gold. One of the little balls and a piece of thread made into a hook are used to fasten the bracelet.

A lovely Urdu verse incorporating a humorous wordplay on the word *paunchi*, which is a homonym of the Urdu word for reached, is as below:

Asks the husband:

> *Jo paunchi maine bheji thi wo paunchi tum tak pahunchi hai*
> *Agar pahunchi toh likh bhejo ke paunchi tum tak pahunchi hai*

> (The bracelet I sent for you, did it reach
> If it reached, please write to me that it has reached you)

Replies the wife:

> *Jo paunchi tumne bheji thi wo paunchi mujh tak pahunchi hai*
> *Magar pahunchi toh kya pahunchi, ke pahunche tak nahi pahunchi*

> (The bracelet you sent for me as reached
> But alas, it doesn't fit me like it should, it doesn't reach my wrist)

So, in fact, the word pahunchi has several *mayney*, or meanings, including wrist in this delightful piece of shayari.

Jewellery worn around the neck has even more unique and special names. *Paan haar*, strands of interconnected heart-shaped pieces of gold; *raani haar*, long, several strands of varying lengths, strung together to adorn the wearer across the upper torso in a striking, bold display; *satlarha*, literally a seven-stranded necklace; *gulluband*, a kind of choker made with velvet and textured, polygonal, thin pieces of beaten gold attached to the velvety band; *tauq*, a dramatic, elaborate and stunning necklace that rests proudly on the wearer's breastbone and extends till the start of the collar bones; *navratan haar* or *chandan haar*, several different gems linked together to form a choker-type necklace; *tursi*, solid balls of gold bunched together and suspended from the necklace; *hasli*, a solid, incomplete, horseshoe-shaped circular band that lies close to the neck, thicker in front and gradually thinning out at the sides and nape of the neck; *matarmala*, tiny balls of gold strung together as chains, worn in strands of varying length around the neck, to name just a few. Of course, there is the simple chain or *zanjeer*, in various sizes, thicknesses and lengths, usually with a small pendant shaped like a flower or a heart. Amma tells of a relative whose besotted husband bought her a solid gold chain as long as her height. She wore it daily, winding it four times around her delicate neck, for as long as she lived.

Knitting is a popular winter activity. There are always little booties and tunic sets being knitted for newborns. Everyone knits; some are more adept and make fancy intricate miniature cardigans with *kangoore* along the edges and pretty embroidered flowers on the bodice, but some choose to make practical and plain ones in dark colours to camouflage the inevitable stains, smears and dribble tracks that will eventually form the artwork on the blank canvas. For adults, there are hand-knit jumpers, mufflers, caps that cover your ears, mittens and all sorts of garments being knitted. There is something cosy and adorable about hand-knitted winter-wear, which we fully appreciate only much later in life. The love and care that seem to run through the skeins, the textural wholesomeness, and the special feeling of wearing something made just for you are things I grow to cherish in my later years in the bone-chilling cold of England.

Pure wool, in different colours, comes in stacks of yarn with the paper label running across them. There is talk of ounces, a measure we do not follow, and of *goley* needed for a particular item. Mummy has patterns carefully saved from tattered old copies of *Women's Weekly*. The slender, blonde, white-skinned women proudly model the jumper or cardigan in the accompanying picture, and we excitedly choose our design based solely on the looks of the model wearing it. Sometimes, an outgrown sweater is carefully unravelled, and one of us is made to sit with our hands aloft while the zig-zaggy, crinkled wool is draped around our hands roughly a foot apart. It looks like we are holding an imaginary placard between our rigidly stretched hands. We are admonished if our attention flounders and our hands get lax, which, in my case, inevitably happens, as sitting still is something that does not come naturally to me. Once the unravelled *oon*, or wool, resembles a woolly, fluffy garland, we are free to move. The wool is then carefully and gently hand-washed and left to dry to out take the creases. The garland now becomes a racing circuit, with several lines of wool running in parallel and crowding one another in a woollen oblong, known as *lachhey*. Our misery has not ended just yet. The wool must now be rolled into balls, and like kittens, but with a lot less fun, we get going with the balls of wool. The knitting needles are out now! They make a metallic clickety-clack sound, and our mother and aunts work furiously, while chatting and planning the meals ahead. The multi-tasking involved is astounding, as the patterns are complicated, with several coloured skeins involved, the stitches, *ulta-seedha* and cable, just to name a few—mind-boggling stuff! There are *ferayil* patterns, which we learn much later is a term for the Fair Isle knit. Fair Isle is a Scottish Shetland island, which is famous for its colourful knits and intricate patterns. The knitting needles, more like long metal rods, are grey in colour with a pointy end and a button-like bulbous end on which is written a number. The number signifies the thickness of the needles. Amma is adept at crochet too, which is known by its colloquial *krushiya* in our household. Amma makes beautiful laces, scarves and jumpers with her crochet hook and scraps of leftover wool. One of her favourite things is to make hundreds of small, colourful squares, each the size of a matchbox, and stitch them together like a patchwork quilt to make shawls, bedspreads and small bags for the children. They are like a beautiful mosaic, with a woolly texture, and cost her nothing as she uses bits of wool left over from knitting, collected in a battered old biscuit tin in neat, tight balls. Each square is a unique multi-coloured flower that makes this beautiful, comfortable blanket a unique and exquisitely soft floral cocoon, one that makes you snuggle and purr like a kitten while reading a book.

The bell rings, and it is Qaiser Khala. She has come to check if all is well with her handyman's work. She greets Amma with affection, calling her Ammi and politely asks, 'Yeh *tasallibaqsh kaam kar raha hai?*'

I am lying on my stomach in the dappled sunlight, and I lazily ask my sister, 'What does tasallibaqsh mean?'

My all-knowing sister retorts, 'That's his name, stupid!'

My other sister nods wisely, as do I, chastened.

Our mother overhears this exchange and bursts out laughing. Apparently tasallibaqsh means 'satisfactory' in the proper, grown-up world of Urdu that we are not yet acquainted with. There is much mirth, and this incident places itself firmly in family folklore. We never find out what his actual name is.

Ruqqaiyya Khala comes in soon after, in a flurry of excitement and giggles. She laughs a lot and animatedly relates an exchange she just had with the rickshaw wala while coming to our house. She settles down amidst her flouncy, frilly and many-layered garments and produces a large, covered pot from the cloth bag she is carrying. She is visiting her brother, Haroon Mamu, who lives close by, and today she has come to visit Amma. She is flighty and a bit kooky at the best of times, and over the years we have come to love her for her childlike innocence and good-natured facetiousness. She laughs easily and often, throwing her head back, and tears run down her naturally pink cheeks. She wears her long, wavy hair in a loosely woven braid, the end of which is in a tasselled pink and red silky *chuteela*. She owns a collection of these and loves buying them in fairs and shops, carefully coordinating them with her colourful and floral-patterned clothes. She is also partial to bejewelled hair clips and hair pins decorated with *gota*, or tinsel, and *sitarey*, or sequins. Dozens of glass bangles clink on her soft and plump forearms, interspersed with gold *kangans* and *kadey*, or flat gold bangles. On her feet are delicate silver *paazeb*, or anklets. Her husband dotes on her and brings her *mogra gajrey* (jasmine garlands) to thread through her hair and boxes of her favourite mithai. She munches on these contentedly and admires the freshly painted henna patterns on her hands. She has no children of her own, and so she showers her love and care on all the youngsters in her realm. We will all have lunch together, and Amma persuades Qaiser Khala to stay for lunch too. Qaiser Khala is an academician and is very elegant and soft-spoken. She is dressed in a beige silk sari and drapes a matching shawl artfully around herself. Her hair is styled in a no-nonsense bun, and her jewellery is discrete and barely noticeable She is extremely well-read and teaches Urdu at the university. University events such as retirements and planned cultural events, along with interesting literary news items, are discussed. We are slightly in awe of Qaiser Khala and find her very inspirational. Interestingly, she too hails from Pilibhit, where our father is from. Pilibhit is a small city located in the Rohilkhand area, close to Bareilly.

We all make our way to the chowki. Sakina has made a vegetable dish called mooli ki bhujia (radishes cooked with their leaves; the pale ivory colour of the grated radishes, flecked with the mossy green of the pungent leaves, devoid of the fiery colourwash of turmeric or tomatoes, simply imbued with the smoky heat of a whole red chilli, or two!). We will have this with fresh rotis and arhar dal. Sakina also warms up the saalan that Ruqqaiyya Khala has brought with her. We peer closely at the serving donga. It is a very pink dish! This is chuqandar gosht (beetroot slow-cooked with mutton until tender). We have never eaten it before, so we gingerly serve small portions on our plates. The deep magenta colouring and the earthy flavour of the dish intrigue us. The meat pieces are tender and imbued with a sweetness and freshness that come from the beetroot. The beetroot itself gives up its heart and soul to the meat and lovingly cradles the morsels, akin to a mother sacrificing herself for her children, becoming a thick, deeply flavoursome and tantalizingly textured gravy. It is delicious!

We have previously had alu gosht with chunky potatoes, bhindi gosht (with okra, and slightly mushy ones at that!), turai gosht (with ridge gourd), tamatar gosht (with ripe tomatoes) and even palak gosht (with spinach), but this is a new thing for us. The practice of adding vegetables to meat is not just for taste and texture but also for adding bulk, making it go a long way. Meat is an expensive ingredient, and adding cheaply available vegetables can feed more mouths. It is an economically sound practice, and in keeping with their infinite wisdom, nutritionally better as well, providing fibre and other nutrients. Sometimes, lentils and beans are added as well, for instance, in chaney ki dal gosht.

We eagerly take second helpings, and someone, probably our older brother, cheekily remarks at how tasallibaqsh the dish was.

The entire incident is repeated for Ruqqaiyya Khala's benefit, and she howls with laughter until her eyes start to water. There is much mirth, and it is repeated over and over again. Our faces are the same colour as the chuqandar gosht. It will take us a few years to see the funny side of this incident, but eventually it will happen.

So here's to Ruqqaiyya Khala and her uninhibited and unbridled laughter, magical winter afternoons in the dappled sunshine and cosy knits that embrace and cocoon one in their warmth and softness. One of the many aunts who watched us grow from the time we were babies, throughout our youth and till today with great pride and joy. One who taught us to laugh in the face of adversity and live life to the fullest.

Chuqandar Gosht

½ kg diced mutton, bones included
3 medium-sized beetroots, peeled and grated
1 onion, chopped
2 tbsp cooking oil
½ tsp red chilli powder
1–2 green chillies cut into pieces, depending on heat preferences
3–4 cloves
a finger-sized stick of cinnamon
2 bay leaves
2 tbsp ginger-garlic paste
2 black cardamoms
½ tsp ground black pepper
½ tsp turmeric powder
2 tsp coriander powder
salt to taste

For the garnish:
a fat pinch of garam masala
fresh coriander leaves

Heat the oil in a large, heavy-bottomed pan.

Add the chopped onions and fry until golden.

Add the ginger-garlic paste, chillies and spices. Add a splash of water and fry the paste till the oil separates.

Add the mutton pieces and stir until they are evenly covered with spices.

Cook for about 30 minutes until nearly done.

Add the grated beetroot and cook for a further 20 minutes on low heat, stirring every now and then to check it has not dried or stuck to the pan.

Add very little water from time to time, as this is not a gravy-based dish.

Check the seasoning.

Sprinkle with garam masala and chopped fresh coriander leaves.

~

The mooli ki bhujiya is a dry vegetable preparation made with fresh radish and its leaves. It is not a curry and has a very different texture from other sabzi dishes we have eaten. The cream-coloured radishes, sharp and strong in taste, are offset by flecks of mossy green. The fried garlic and whole red chillies give the dish a very earthy, smoky and intense vibe.

Mooli ki Bhujiya

1 mooli (radish) with leaves

4 cloves of garlic
2 whole red chillies
½ tsp red chilli powder
1–2 green chillies, finely chopped
1 tbsp cooking oil
salt as required

First wash, scrape and chop the mooli into small pieces. Chop the washed leaves too.

Add the chopped vegetables to a large pot half-filled with water and bring to a boil. Once cool, drain and squeeze out the water. Set aside.

In a *karahi*, or wok, heat the oil, and add finely sliced garlic and whole red chillies. As soon as the garlic changes colour to a very pale beige, add the cooked radish and leaves.

Lower the heat and add the red chilli powder, green chillies and salt. Sauté it all together until well-cooked and dry.

Serve with roti and any kind of dal.

~

Laughter is the best medicine. And, of course, with Ruqqaiyya Khala, there was plenty of that. There were many other humorous and witty family members, and we listened to their anecdotes and jokes with great interest. As children, this laughter and humour were part of the warmth and nurturing that taught us to deal with problems and navigate awkward social situations. Those anecdotes became so familiar that it seemed as though we had actually been there. Now we retell these to our children during cosy nostalgic conversations during long wintry evenings, in lands far, far away . . .

Mere suraj aa, mere jism pe apna saaya kar
Badhi tez hava hai, sardi aaj ghazab ki hai

—Shahryar

(O Sun, come and warm my body with your rays
The wind is strong and it is bitterly cold today)

Azeemuddin's Istoo

Azeemuddin had been the cook in Amma's home since long before I was born, and he served the household for many, many years. He first arrived as a young boy when my grandmother got married and set up home as a young bride. Soon after, my mother and her two brothers were born, all of whom were cared for and fed by him. He continued serving the household with dedication, politeness and good humour until he was old and unwell and wished to return to his village to pass the twilight years of his life. My grandmother cared for him like she would a family member and relied on his opinion and expertise on various household matters. There was nothing that he couldn't do—a real Man Friday, or *mushkil kusha* (the trouble-vanquisher), as many called him.

Not only was he an expert and calm cook who did not baulk at the prospect of cooking for dozens of visitors at very short notice, he could also be relied upon to take gold jewellery such as rings and bracelets for repair to the local sunaar, do the grocery shopping, and in the days before telephones, act as an emissary with important messages within and outside the extended family. He was treated with great respect by the youngsters who were in his charge. Amma, for her part, made sure his children were educated and helped him arrange their weddings too. His daughter Shakila had wanted a *bulakhh*, a nose ring that hangs from the central septum of the nose, reaching the 'V' of the upper lip, swinging gently and suspended majestically as a focal point of the face. It was a stunning piece of jewellery, not commonly seen by the more sophisticated city dwellers of my mother's generation. It was more common for brides to wear a more traditional *nath*, a large ring in the piercing of the left nostril, either festooned with a delicate gold chain or a string of tiny pearls. My mother never had her nose pierced and did not wear one at her wedding, but Amma did and had a large diamond nose stud that she wore all the time. As for Shakila, she had her bulaakh, along with other jewellery befitting a bride, and gorgeous clothes too; Amma saw to it. The sons were helped to get suitable jobs, and Azeemuddin was content with his lot. When my older siblings were born, he was again at hand, nurturing, feeding and helping run the household though he was getting older and weaker. My older siblings remember him very well, though I have faint memories of a wiry, talkative elderly gentleman with a beard, dressed in a white kurta and Aligarh-cut pyjama, who was not only an excellent cook but also affectionate, humorous and polite. He doted on my older sister, always saving tasty tidbits and treats for her while playfully admonishing my brother for his mischief! They called him Muddi Baba, and he would address all of us girls as Bibi. We used to find it so amusing that he continued to address our father as *dulha miyan* (the bridegroom), long after his marriage to our mother, several children and well into middle age!

As for me, a succession of ayahs was sent by Amma from Aligarh, as, by then, our family had moved to Delhi and Mummy had started to work. Obviously, I have little or no memory of those women, but Fareedan's name features prominently, more for her incompetence and laziness than for anything positive and praiseworthy! She was sent packing, of course.

I remember my younger sister's ayah a lot better. Her name was Bauwa, and she was a diminutive old lady, clad in faded cotton saris with an *ulta palla*, where the palla, or end of a sari, goes around the back and shoulder to cover the front part of the body, the edges skimming over the stomach area and tucked in the waistband in front. The usual sari palla goes diagonally across the front, and the free edge sways gracefully behind the wearer, covering her head. Underneath, she wore an oversized men's shirt, faded and possibly handed down from her son, buttoned up to her much too thin neck, and limp collars that curled at the edges like a child drawing the waves of the sea in their art book. She wore a large brass nose stud and had a tattoo in Hindi on her wrinkled forearm that said 'Ram'. She was a devout Hindu woman from a small village near Aligarh and had been brought to stay with us by her son, Ramavtar, who worked as a clerk in Abba's office in the University. Being a very pious lady, she made her own *choolha* (makeshift stove) in the corner of our *aangan* (courtyard) and placed her own utensils and pans nearby. She had a small room to herself, too. She was a strict vegetarian and would not eat or drink anything from our house, as we were meat eaters. We were forewarned that she was very particular about her *shudh* (pure) surroundings, and it was best not to disturb that sanctity. All of us children were told not to touch her *gharha* (earthenware pot) of water or any of her belongings. Of course, her charge, my little sister, clung to her like a limpet at most times, and these restrictions did not apply to her. We were amused to hear her sigh 'Hai morey Ramuva' as she would get up from a squatting position, an expression our little sister too started saying, possibly one of her earliest sentences. Such was her fondness and affection for my little sister that she cradled her to sleep every night, humming old Bhojpuri lullabies, and cared for her tirelessly and with staunch dedication. A neighbourhood woman in the local park once remarked tartly about my sister being the third girl child and how unfortunate that was. A much-incensed Bauwa famously retorted, 'Jaun Ram diyain uhi toh howat, tumhaar ho to tum khud hi garh lena. Hamaar chunnoo toh sau betwa pe bhaari hain! (Whatever Ram ji gives us, will come to us. When it is your turn, you can manufacture what you like. Our girl is better than a hundred sons). This incident was later related to my mother by her, and our father, a champion of girl power, was greatly amused and impressed by her spirited answer!

All of us had great respect for her and her beliefs and made sure she had her own space and the freedom to practise her faith with dignity. Even so, sometimes the peace was inadvertently shattered, either by a stray cat or my brother's bulldog, Tintin, usually being the culprit, and this usually quiet and gentle old lady transformed into a raging, screaming ball of fury. She was possessed by Bhavaani, we were told. In the open aangan, she would start to sway and contort herself, muttering gibberish, her arms flailing and her hair, usually invisible under the sari head covering, and neatly tied in a bun, would be loose and in a state of disarray. Her eyes would look wild, almost haunted. She would stamp her feet on the concrete and moan loudly. In due course, it would all subside. We all knew to keep out of her way. This happened very rarely and did not traumatize or scare us in the least, even though it sounds terrifying. We respected her and accepted this occurrence as part of who she was. She would then lay down, spent and weary, recover and everything would return to normalcy. Mummy would inquire gently, 'Theek ho Bauwa?' She would nod her head and busy herself immediately. She never harmed herself or anybody else, and she stayed with us for several years until her charge was ready to go to school. She went back to stay with her son and his wife and some years later, passed away peacefully.

While Azeemuddin was adept at making the proper khansama kind of fare such as qorma, pasandey (flattened fillet cuts of marinated meat cooked in a gravy until tender and flavoursome), paayey (trotters, slow cooked in a thin gravy considered a delicacy by some, a variation being siri-paye, or the head and feet of the goat or sheep cooked together), nargisi koftey (a hard-boiled egg encased in a shell of qeema or mince, similar to the British scotch egg, but served in a thin gravy) and murgh musallam (a whole chicken cooked in its entirety) and of course all sorts of biryani and pulao dishes and a plethora of kebabs, to name just a few, his lasting legacy has got to be his famous 'istoo'. Istoo, of course, is the Urdu word for stew, and much like the words school, smile or starters, it has an 'I' sound at its beginning when spoken by an Urdu speaker.

Like many of the English words used and adapted to their own language, there are many words that have their origins in the days of British colonialism. The words for hospital, cycle, glass and plate were all adapted for use in common parlance, with minor variations. It is amusing to note that there are Urdu words for most of the cutlery like forks, knives and spoons (kaanta, chhuri and chammach), which probably were not in use earlier, but a plate is usually called just a plate. A shallow bowl-like rakaabi perhaps, a baadhiya, or a tray-like tashtari, are other similar vessels. In my mother's childhood, they ate in taamba, or copper plates, with regular *qalai* to keep them pristine. A glass or tumbler to drink from became *gilaas*. A bottle, usually a glass one, became *botal* and a smaller one became *shishi*. The place for higher education, a college, became *kaalij*. The great game of cricket became *kirkit*. And where would tea be in the present day without *biskut* (biscuits)? As many of the fabrics for clothes came from England and were very popular, these too were adapted to everyday Urdu usage. These include *saatan* (satin), *shamoo saatan* (chamois satin), *jaarjat* (georgette) and *chheent* (chintz), to name a few. Of course, it was a two-way street, as many English words have Urdu origins, like cummerbund, jungle, shampoo, loot, thug and pyjamas, to name just a few.

The British rule left its *chhaap* (mark) in countless ways, both good and bad. The quintessential practice of tea drinking is common to both the British and the Indian subcontinent. Where would we be without tea?

In Amma's home, of course, tea was an elaborate affair, with *ehtemaam* and *saleekha* (fanfare and precision) at *shaam ki chai* (evening tea) in particular. Loose tea leaves were used to brew the tea in an old Muradabadi teapot. Boiling hot water was used to rinse and warm up the teapot and then poured over the tea leaves. The lid was replaced, and a tea cosy was placed over the full teapot to keep it warm. Of course, Amma fashioned a tea cosy from scraps of white fabric, stuffed with cotton to make a D-shaped hat-like structure, and covered it with a daintily embroidered tea cosy cover. This could be taken off and washed whenever needed. Matching the tea cosy was a fabric tray cover. Usually a lace edging, crocheted by Amma, would form the *kangoore*, or scalloping edges, and there would be hand-embroidered roses or daisies on the cloth itself. The tray itself was a large and heavy Muradabadi, intricately embossed metal tray, with only the generous, curved handles visible from under the tray cloth. Over the tray nestled a matching milk jug, or *doodhdaan*, with a wide spout and hot milk in it. A *shakardaan*, or sugar pot, with granulated sugar and a matching little spoon completed the set. For everyday use, we had a plethora of mix-and-match cups in various shapes, sizes and colours. The shaam ki chai warranted bone china tea cups and matching saucers with delicate pastel floral patterns. Usually, two or three snack items accompanied the tea, of which at least one was sweet. This could be a halwa of some sort, suji, lauki or gajar. The savoury element was more often than not crispy, ajwain-laden, khhasta namak parey, diamond-shaped and crisp maida snacks, fried green peas spiked with crushed black pepper, finely chopped green chillies and cumin seeds, simply called hari matar in winter or mini samosas filled with qeema or a spicy potato mixture. A leisurely 4 p.m. affair, not to be rushed, and something to keep one fed from lunch until dinner later in the night.

Tea is the backbone of social interactions in the Indian subcontinent, and even the most casual visitor is always asked if they would like to have tea, whatever time of the day. In countless homes, offices and train stations, one is only a few minutes away from a piping hot cup of tea, with minor regional variations. It is an essential feature of our lives, punctuating the wakeful hours, soothing our souls and oiling the machinery of life, easing all tribulations and turmoil with its comforting warmth and sweetness. Along with the newspapers, a cup of tea marks the beginning of most urban households.

Ghee misri bhi bhej kabhi akhbaron mein
Kaee dinon se chai hai kadwi ya Allah

—Nida Fazli

(Please send good things in the newspapers
The bitterness ruins my tea, O Allah)

Amma sometimes makes a large batch of sev to store and enjoy with the evening tea. Vast quantities are made, as these last well if stored in a tin or airtight box. It involves making a large quantity of besan dough spiked with red chillies and seasoned well with salt, cumin and ajwain. An ancient-looking tool with multiple attachments is brought out. It resembles a large metal syringe, looking like something out of a medieval torture chamber. We are asked to assist, and soon there are mounds of noodle-like sev, crisp and intensely savoury-smelling. We wait for them to cool down and transfer them to the various cleaned and dried containers, eagerly wolfing down a few while doing so. The different attachments are for different thicknesses and shapes of the sev. Ribbed or plain, star-shaped along their circumference, or thick and short ones, studded with kalonji, or Nigella seeds, there are lots to savour.

Sometimes Amma makes a sweet version of namak para, known as shakar parey or gurh parey, made with sugar or jaggery, respectively, and sometimes til ke laddoo, especially during the winter months. Shakar parey are chunks of deep-fried dough enrobed in a dry white sugar coating, while the gur ones are caramel-coloured and glisten with the earthy goodness of melted jaggery.

Coming back to the phenomenal istoo, it is somewhat different from the western concept of stew, though it does involve slow-cooking fairly large pieces of meat on the bone (botis). The difference is the large quantity of sliced onions and whole spices (kharha masala) that are used. Neither coriander powder nor turmeric or tomatoes are used, as is conventionally done for a saalan, or curry; there are no fancy cashews or almonds to thicken the gravy. There is not even the ubiquitous first step that is vital for making any great curry dish, the browning or caramelization of onions. Therein lies its difference from the usual saalan or meat curry dish, as most people know it. There is no prepared masala paste; things are simply thrown together with a couple of whole red dried chillies and simmered to a tender, wholesome and intensely pleasurable creation.

This is soul food; it nourishes the body and soothes the mind. There is a definite but not unwelcome sweetness to the dish, brought about by the copious amounts of onion used and also by the mellow and woody hints of sweetness from the pieces of cinnamon sticks. But the sweetness does not jar; it feels right and is brilliantly offset by the fiery red chillies. The cooked onions, with their voluptuous ooziness, also cradle the meat chunks in their midst, rendering them juicy, pillowy and full of enticing promise. The meat, tender and flavoursome, simply falls off the bone with the merest tug. A touch of creamy yoghurt or curd towards the end gives it a hint of tartness and perfectly balances the dish, taking it to a sublime, almost celestial level. Its colour is gloriously amber, neither a fiery red such as tamatar gosht nor a deep, sumptuous bhuna-gosht-brown and most certainly not the turmeric-laden yellow of alu gosht. The aroma is indescribable—a heady mix of warm whole spices, masses of sweetly tender garlic and the robust earthiness of ginger. It is a simple dish to make but very difficult to get absolutely right. Even the reckless, thrown-together recipe calls for finesse, expertise and that obscure yet magical talent known as *andaaz*, or skilful estimation.

There are many happy memories of eating this at my grandparents' home, then my parents and now my own. Eaten simply with alu ke warq and warm roti, this is one of the most life-affirming, comforting and magical meals ever. I wish I could say that I can replicate Azeemuddin's istoo in my London kitchen but that would be very far from the truth. At the end of the day, even if we follow the recipe accurately and use the finest, freshest and most authentic ingredients we can find, there is always that immeasurable and intangible difference, and that is down to the *haath ka mazaa*, or the cook's refinement (literally, the taste attributable to the cook's hands!). That is something that mere mortals like us can only aspire to—something that makes the difference between an average sportsperson and a champion! So here's to Azeemuddin's skilful hands, his culinary expertise, humour, dedication and his lasting legacy, this magnificent istoo.

Istoo

In the olden days, a *degh* (large pot) would be used, but it is absolutely fine to use a pressure cooker or any sort of slow cooker. The idea is to place all the ingredients in like strangers at a party and let them get to know one another, mingling, opening up and releasing their hidden qualities, bringing out the best in each other and coming together to form a glorious, harmonious conglomerate, of course, while gently simmering in a pot.

250 gm lamb or mutton, meat on the bone, cut into fairly similar-sized chunks
2–3 medium to large sized onions, chopped, roughly similar in weight to the meat
4 cloves of garlic
2-inch piece of ginger, sliced
1 bay leaf
1–2 large whole dried red chilli

1 tbsp cooking oil
½ tsp cumin seeds
3-4 peppercorns
a small stick of cinnamon
1 whole clove
2 black cardamoms
salt to taste
½ tsp garam masala
2 tbsp curd or plain yoghurt

Heat the oil in a heavy-bottomed pot or pressure cooker, and add the cumin seeds.

When they splutter, carefully add all the other ingredients: the whole spices first, then the onion, ginger and garlic, finally the meat. No water is needed as the onions will release their moisture, cooking the meat in it.

Give it a gentle stir to mix the ingredients and close the lid tightly.

Cook on low heat for about 40-50 minutes, depending on the size of the meat pieces.

Check that the meat is done; it should fall off the bone with the gentle tug of a fork. Turn the heat off.

Mix the curd or yoghurt in a bowl until it is smooth and paste-like. Add it to the pot and very gently fold it in.

Check the seasoning, sprinkle the garam masala, and transfer to a serving bowl.

Best served with hot roti and alu ke warq, and out of this world with some sheermal.

~

The haath ka maza is common to all home cooks celebrated in this book. And that ultimately comes down to a passion for and deep understanding of food and cooking. One who thinks of cooking as not a chore or a dreary hardship but as an act of love, a badge of pride, a desire to please and soothe, and a gift for those we cherish.

Food not only nourishes our bodies but also our souls and minds. It connects us to our pasts, our roots and childhoods. It is deeply intertwined with nostalgia; the mere smell of seekh kebabs sends me into raptures, encapsulating those idyllic days of Aligarh. The sight of mangoes piled up in carts of vendors, the sound of dough being kneaded, and the feel of biting into a spongy rasgulla are all evocative of happy times in the past for me. They magically transport me to that place, that time and that age of my youth, wherever in the world I may be. Similarly, a simple meal of khichdi, with the crisped onion slices redolent with the aroma of ghee, a bowl of maash ki dal with warm roti or a hearty khichda with slivers of ginger strewn on top, all evoke the times spent with extended family, times of laughter, banter and retelling of *qisse* (stories). Or of having a mound of steaming tahiri (a spicy, vibrantly hued rice dish with chunks of potatoes) and freshly fried shami kebab, with a raita on the side. Azeemudin, sadly, has long gone, as have many others mentioned here. Just as we remember them fondly, I would like to think that they too gaze affectionately from their place in heaven, reminiscing and very pleased with the fact that we still remember them with great love and affection. Generations later, they still have ownership of these dishes that they once loved to cook for others.

Dar-o-deewar pe hasrat se nazr kartein hain
Khush raho ahle-e-vatan hum to safar kartein hain

                      —Nawab Wajid Ali Shah, Akhtar

(I gaze at the door and the walls with a sense of longing
Stay happy, my countrymen, I must leave)

Shahida Chachi's Spectacular Rasawal

Shahida Chachi is from Lucknow, the city of nawabs, famous for its elaborate and sumptuous feasts, finesse in speech and manner, and the epitome of refined tastes in food and lifestyles. And Shahida Chachi is true to her provenance. She cooks fabulous meals and is eager to share her culinary creations with us. She is extremely well spoken, tall, statuesque and elegant, dressed in understated silk saris in muted colours, preferring plain cotton ones with perhaps a contrasting darker shaded border in the summer. She often hosts a *daawat* (feast) at her house, with tasteful crockery and lavish-sounding dishes, many of which are unfamiliar to us. She regales all with tales of nawabs attempting to outdo one another in refinement, asking their cooks to peel individual peas and stuff the *chhilka*, or covering, of each tiny pea with qeema as a re-imagined qeema matar or nargisi koftey made with quail eggs and the finest venison. Our young minds try in vain to comprehend the elaborate preparation of such indulgent and fanciful foods. We wonder at the time and effort it must have taken the poor cooks and kitchen staff to perform such intricate and complex culinary feats on a daily basis.

Shahida Chachi's children are roughly our age, and we are friends with them. She is married to Abba's younger brother, Professor Aulad Ahmad, who teaches Economics at the University and is extremely learned and intellectual. Even though she is our mother's chachi, they are roughly the same age and are great friends. So her children, though cousins of our mother, have a sort of friendly sibling-like bond with us. It feels like we are cousins, and duly refer to one another by our first names. Apart from long sessions of Scrabble, Ludo, Snakes and Ladders and cards, we share a love of food and have long, animated discussions on various mithais, cakes, kebabs, pastries and other delectable treats. The feast served at a family wedding, a new eatery or the fare served at the Numaish (an annual Aligarh fair) are all topics of great interest to us.

We have been invited to a rasawal party by Shahida Chachi, and we all duly arrive at her immaculately neat house. She has a beautiful and exquisite collection of crockery, and we all sit together at and around the dining table. Rasawal is more of a rural preparation, made with fresh sugar cane juice known as ganne ka ras, hence the name. It is a seasonal delicacy regularly prepared in urban homes too, when sugar cane is in season. We also love to eat fresh, peeled sugar cane, sold on wooden carts, or thelas, cut into roughly lemon-sized chunks, piled on slabs of ice to keep them cool, and strewn with rose petals. We chew the cylindrical, luscious pieces, known as ganderi, till we have extracted all the juice and a dry, fibrous pulp remains that we spit out in a bin. Sometimes, we drink glasses full of freshly squeezed juice and watch excitedly as bunches of long, bamboo-like sugar cane are passed in between two large steel wheels, rotating simultaneously, one atop the other. A frothy, pale green, intensely sweet and refreshing juice comes out from a spout at the side, collected in jugs and poured into glasses. These are the only two ways that we've had ganna until now.

Assembling the extended family for a special, traditional and, more importantly, seasonal food item is not an uncommon thing. One who takes pride in and ownership of this particular dish would invite several people from the extended family who lived nearby, and it would generally be an informal, casual event. No fancy table settings but, rather a large *dastarkhwan*, or thick cloth used as a serving mat for people to sit around, cross-legged on a durrie or carpet-clad floor or a large chowki. This could be special and authentic meat dishes like khichda or haleem, shabdegh, paaye, or simply seasonal delicacies like boot pulao (a pulao made with rice and tender green chickpeas, known as boot), kali gajar ka halwa, amras (a dish made with unripe mangoes and semolina, said to protect one against the killer Loo winds or a sunstroke) or simply masses of mangoes that came from one's own orchard. Sometimes there would be picnics in scenic spots where everyone cooked and brought along something they made well, like a potluck. These could be alu puri, roghani tikiyan, shami kebab, halwa or shakar parey. One of the elders in the family, whom my mother refers to as Chhoti Dadi, did an annual daawat for the extended family with a one-pot menu. This was the *hannda* (a large pot) that was set upon a *choolha* (makeshift stove) in the courtyard and had several kilos of meat cooked with all kinds of leafy green vegetables or saag she could get hold of, seasonal, of course. It simmered on a low heat all night, and the next morning, she laid out her favourite dastarkhwan, a large yellow fabric sheet with various shers hand-embroidered on it. Everyone sat around it on the massive chowki and ate this special and wholesome saalan with fresh tandoori roti bought from a local tandoor. No other dishes were served, and it was an annual ritual that everyone looked forward to. There was no dessert as such, perhaps seasonal fruit for people to help themselves to, but usually she made a platter of *lauzaat*, or sweet treat. She used to collect the seeds of melons for several months in anticipation of this daawat. She painstakingly washed, dried and peeled these, cooked them with sugar and made barfi-shaped tidbits as a post-meal lauzaat.

More stories about delectable treats from the olden days sold by hawkers or at halwai shops are told. My grandmother reminisces about lauki ke taar, which sounds very exotic and is not something we would associate with the bland and bulbous elongated bottle gourds we turn up our noses at! Delicately grated, long juliennes of lauki, or bottle gourd, fragranced with kewra (pandanus) are spun in sugar, magically transforming them into the noodle-like treats that she enjoyed as a girl. Another unusual and elaborate childhood treat for her was malai ki gilauri. Layers of the cream from milk, or malai, were constructed to form a triangular shape resembling a paan, shaped and ready to be eaten, and stuffed with khoya, nuts and dried fruit. Like so many things, these forgotten foods have vanished, either due to a lack of demand, evolving tastes and palates or the complexities of production.

Amma tells stories of the celebration of Saawan, or the month of rains, called Saawani, which she and her own cousins were invited to in their youth. Usually, an older woman in the family, a khala, chachi, tai or phupi would take the initiative of organizing and preparing the food and other special things required. These were the *jhooley* (swings) on the trees in the orchards, usually the branches of sturdy mango trees; gifts of pastel green glass bangles, known as *kareliyan* and hand-crinkled *mulmul* dupattas in pastel colours for all the young girls of the family. The foods that were made on these occasions have such quaint and evocative names: andarse (sweet, fried and crisp sesame-encrusted treats); arbi ke patte ke pakode (arbi or colocasia leaves, washed and spread with a spicy chickpea flour mixture, rolled up, steamed, cut into discs and fried); dal bhari pooriyan, also called berahi; dal bhari kachori; rasbhariyan (deep-fried dough balls dipped in a thick syrup); lauki ke taar (grated bottle gourd dipped in a thick syrup), dahi ki phulkiyan; and angoor ke patton ki phulki (made with young, fresh leaves from the grapevine, served with fiery red chilli and garlic chutney).

The rains were such a magical time for those who lived and eked a living tilling the land in the dusty, parched and arid areas of the plains of Uttar Pradesh. A harsh, prolonged and merciless summer season finally came to an end, and with it went the terror of the killer Loo winds, dried-up lakes and rivers, and dying cattle. The rains not only brought a promise of revival, vibrancy and sustenance but also of joy and aesthetic pleasure. The sondhi (fragrant) smell of the thirsty soil when it gets its first drink of pure rainwater, the petrichor, is a joy to experience! A lot of traditional folk songs celebrated this and painted a picture of renewed life, of peacocks dancing unfettered, of koel birds calling out from lush grasslands and of blooming perfumed flowers. Saawan was the month of the arrival of rain, a gift from the sky, baarish for some, megha for others. A gentle phuhaar here, a dramatic show of lightening called bijli or bijuria there, dark menacing clouds somewhere else, kaley baadal or karey badariya, accompanied by a loud garaj (bellow) in all its glorious forms. The month signalled the arrival of plentiful and torrential rains, a welcome respite to the parched, bone-dry earth and a magic wand that turned an arid wasteland into a glistening, vibrant haven for all.

As Saawan was such a special and life-affirming month, it was natural to have songs that welcomed and celebrated it. *Saawan ke geet* or *gaane* were an integral part of all the celebrations that accompanied it. Most of the Saawan songs that were sung by the young girls in those times had a simple, rustic charm and evoked lush greenery, contrasting with *birhaa*, or being away from their beloved, or the longing for their *maika*, or maternal home, if married. Many married women were able to go to their parental home, escorted by a male relative, of course!

This simple and delightful song is about a young married woman wondering which of her male relatives from her parental home is going to send a *doli* (palanquin), a form of transport in the olden days that had the woman sitting in a box-like compartment with curtains to shield her from prying eyes and a roof to protect her from the elements. There were four people carrying that compartment, holding the poles that stuck out from it. An elaborate and ornate one was also the preferred method of transport for brides to travel to their marital homes.

> *Neem ki nimkoli pakki saawan mein koi aayega*
> *Jeeve meri ma ka jaya doli bhej bulaega*
> *Neem ki nimkoli pakki saawan mein koi aayega*
> *Jeeve mera mamu acchha doli bhej bulaega*

> (The Neem tree has borne fruit, in this season someone will come
> My mother's son (brother) will send a doli for me to come home
> The Neem tree has borne fruit, in this season someone will come
> My mother's brother will send a doli for me to come home)

And so on, citing all the older male relatives on her parental side—chacha, tau, khalu, etc.—and wistfully wondering who will bring her home.

The *jhoola*, or a swing hanging from a branch of a tree, is an oft-repeated motif, a symbol of joy and exhilaration from feeling the cool, fresh breeze on one's cheek, and a playful activity enjoyed with other young girls. Usually, one girl stands behind the girl seated on the swing, pushing her forward so that the swing moves higher and faster. This action of pushing is called *jhotey*. Sometimes the swing is decorated with the abundant and fragrant flowers from the garden, further increasing the aesthetic charm and enjoyment of swaying on the swing. The tinkling sounds of the colourful glass bangles, the dupatta fluttering in the wind and the luxuriously soft feel of the silken threads or string that are braided together to make the ropes of the swing gentle to the touch, are all the components that enhance the simple child-like activity, and these accompanying songs capture these beautifully. The sweet and evocative song made popular in the film *Junoon* captures these moments beautifully, paints an idyllic picture of the rains and uses imagery and rural dialect to convey innocence and joy:

Ghir aai kari ghata matwari
Saawan ki aai bahaar re
Bela chameli ki kaliyan chatak gayin
Mehkat ban ki bayaar re
Khil gaye hatheli pe mehndi ke bootey
Lachkat jhoolan se daal
Dhani chunar mere sar pe na thehre
Chhoodiyan karey jhankaar re

(The joyful clouds of rain are here
The month of rains have brought forth beauty
The flowers of jasmine are in bloom
And the air of the forest is fragrant
The floral patterns of henna are painted on palms
The swings made the branches of trees sway
My pale green scarf slips away from my head
And my glass bangles clink merrily)

And another simple folk song describes the action of putting up a swing:

Jhoola dala suhawna resham dori ko batt ke
Jhooley pe baithi rani pyari
Jhoola dala suhawana resham dori ko batt ke
Sakhiyon se kahe rani pyari
Jhotey dena sambhaal ke mori chunri na atke

(We have put up a beautiful swing with silken ropes
A lovely girl sits on it
She says to her friends
Careful, do not push too forcefully, lest my scarf gets entangled)

Another rural folk song is a playful ditty about a woman imploring her husband to get the henna for her to decorate her hands with:

Piya mehdi liyana moti jheel se
Jai ke saikeel pe
Chhoti nandi se piswana seel pe
Hum lagay lebe kaanta aur keel se

(O husband, bring me some fresh henna leaves from Moti Jheel.*
Go on your bicycle
Get your little sister to grind it by hand on a stone
And then I will decorate my hands with fine patterns using thorns and nails)

There are some more sweet folk songs about Saawan, with minor regional variations, as one travels along the hinterlands of Uttar Pradesh, the language taking on a more Bhojpuri dialect and references.

Ghan ghan garje badarwa
cham cham chamke bijuriya
Badra karey na bauchhar sawan

(The clouds are rumbling
The lightning shines brightly
But no rains, not even a drizzle)

Jhoola dalo ri sakhi sawan aayo
Rimjhim meha barse
Dil mora jhoomjhoom jaye

(O friend of mine, put up the swing on a tree, the rains are here
The raindrops fall gently
And my heart sways with joy)

---

* Moti Jheel is beautiful garden situated near Kanpur and built during the British rule.

Sakhi ri maine jhoola dala hai bagian mein
Resham ki toh main dor le aai
Chandi ki maine paazeb banwayi
Sakhi ri maine kar liye solah singaar
Sakhi ri maine jhoola dala hai bagian mein

(O friend, I have put up a swing in the garden
I have got silken strings for the rope
I have got silver anklets made
I have adorned myself with cosmetics
O friend)

The friends play together on swings, expressing their thoughts and enjoying the season:

Jhooley parh gaye daari daari
Naachey man ka mor sakhi ri
Saawan hai ghanghor sakhi ri

(The swings are hanging from various branches of trees
My heart dances with joy like a peacock, O friend
It is raining heavily, O friend)

Ari behna thar thar toh kaampe mera dil
Haule se jhotey de mujhe
Champa chaman main to jhoolti
Ari bibi jhoole saheliyon ke sath
Haule se jhotey de mujhe
Nanhi nanhi boondey parh rahin
Hauley se jhotey de mujhe

(O sister, my heart trembles
Push me gently on the swing
I am delicate like flowers
Push me gently on the swing
Tiny droplets fall from the sky
Push me gently on the swing)

Another beautiful melody with its rain-drenched, impassioned plea to a beloved, imploring them to visit. It paints a picture of longing for a love that was pure and deep but has now been forgotten by someone.

Baghon mein padhe jhooley
Tum bhool gaye humko
Hum tumko nahi bhoole
Yeh raqs sitaron ka
Sun lo kabhi afsana
Taqdeer ke maron ka
Saawan ka mahina hai
Sajan se juda reh kar
Jeena bhi kya jeena hai
Raavi ka kinara hai
Har mauj ke hothon par afsana hamara hai
Ab aur na tadpao, ya humko bula bhejo
Ya aap chaley aao

Birhaa is a genre of songs of longing for a beloved who, for whatever reason, is unable to be by her side. The romance of the raindrops, the lush greenery and fragrant flowers like bela and chameli only heighten the sense of distance, gloom and longing for the beloved. *Kajri*, a similar genre of songs, also echoes these sentiments.

Many newly married young women visit their maika and for those for whom this is not possible, it is a tearful, tragic and frustrating time. In this very popular and evocative song, full of longing and sadness, a young married woman pleads with her mother to send someone to fetch her and take her back home for the Saawan season, but the mother makes excuses and explains why she must stay.

> *Amma merey babul ko bhejo ri*
> *Ke saawan aaya, ke saawan aaya*

She first asks her mother to send her father, who is too frail to travel. Then she asks for her brother, but he is a mere boy and cannot come. Finally, she asks for her childhood back, but the mother says that too has long gone.

The noted Urdu playwright and poet, Agha Hashr Kashmiri in his book *Asir-e-Hirs* also paints an idyllic and evocative picture with these jhooley songs.

> *Amwa ki dari taley aao ri*
> *Jhoolna jhulao ri*
> *Bhole piya sang dharhkey umang*
> *Jhooloon jhulaoon*
> *Resham ki dori bandha di*
> *Amwa ki dari taley aao ri*

> (Come, beneath the branches of the mango tree
> Come and push me on the swing
> I can savour the joyous time with my sweet beloved

I can swing and also push the swing
The silken threads are tied on the swing
Come, beneath the branches of the mango tree

And another one sung by the *saheliyan*, or friends:

Jhooley wali hai Rashke gul e lala jhoola
Ja ke bulbul tu rag e gul ka bana la jhoola
Aaj dikhlayega andaz nirala jhoola
Chaand pyari hai to ban jayega haala jhoola

(The beauty who sits on the swing is the envy of the poppy
flower
O nightingale, go and make a swing with the delicate veins of
the flower
The swing will show us its glory and uniqueness
If our friend is the moon, the swing is its halo)

Rasawal

Fresh sugar cane juice is cooked with rice, carefully skimming off
the impurities while stirring it. The rice used is short grain, broken,
and not basmati. Served with ice-cold milk or malai in summers
and with hot milk as a warming treat in winters. Skimming off the
scum from the juice as it cooks gives a lighter colour to the finished
rasawal. It's traditionally poured into a large, wide earthenware pot
and left to set for a while before savouring.

1 cup ordinary broken rice, soaked
3 litres sugar cane juice
1 tbsp grated desiccated coconut

1 black cardamom
milk, to serve

Take a large pot and boil the sugar cane juice, skimming off the impurities or scum that forms using a spatula.

Keep skimming it off while it cooks on a low flame and reduces, then add the soaked rice to it, along with the cardamom.

Cover the pot and simmer further for about an hour, or until it looks like a thick porridge in consistency.

Mix it well and let it cool. Set in an earthenware large pot, sprinkling the coconut on top.

Serve warm or cold, depending on the weather, with some milk poured on top.

Shahida Chachi has strewn some fresh rose petals from her garden on the rasawal, along with small slices of dried coconut, and it looks sensational, with the smell from the earthenware mingling with the heady-smelling desi rose petals. It has been a very convivial and delightful brunch, and we have tried a new dish.

Patorey is another dish she makes with great pride and zeal.

Patorey are made from the fresh leaves of arbi, or colocasia, which grows just under the surface of the ground. The vibrant, emerald green, satiny leaves look like elegant little canopies. The leaves are plucked fresh for use and rinsed thoroughly. They are then encased in a spicy batter and steamed. These are made very frequently when the leaves are abundant.

Patorey

Makes about 6
6–8 fresh arbi leaves

4 tsp besan (chickpea flour)
1 tsp ginger-garlic paste
salt to taste
a pinch of ajwain or carom seeds
½ tsp roasted cumin powder
½ tsp red chilli powder
a little oil for frying
black peppercorns, freshly ground
lime wedges

Wash the leaves carefully and dry them on a clean kitchen cloth.

In a mixing bowl, add the besan, spices and a little water. The batter should be quite thick, like plaster, so add water little by little. Mix thoroughly to avoid any lumps.

Place a leaf on a large, flat plate and smoothly coat it with the batter. Keep alternating until it is a few layers thick. Reserve some of the batter.

Roll the layers carefully into a log or sausage shape, and carefully apply the remaining batter to the outer surface of the roll.

Tie with thread on either side and carefully place the plate in a steamer. Alternatively, you can use a large, covered pan with a little water at the bottom and an upturned metal bowl under the plate. Steam for 15 minutes.

Carefully, take the rolled-up log out and let it cool.

Slice into thick discs with a sharp knife while holding the log in place.

Take some oil in a frying pan and carefully shallow fry the discs, showing spirals of yellow and green.

Serve with freshly ground black pepper and lime wedges.

~

The celebrations we have in the present day are so different from those in our youth, even more so going back a few generations. Religious festivals and weddings aside, we now tend to celebrate birthdays, anniversaries, moving houses and job advancements. We invite our friends, share food with them or go out for a meal. Back then, it could be a celebration of the arrival of a season, the mango season, a child's completion of the reading of the Quran or their first solid meal. But the concept is the same. Sharing good times, marking an event, bringing people together and making memories.

> *Basant aai hai mauj e rang-e-gul hai josh-e-sahbaa hai*
> *Khuda ke fazl se aish-o-tarab ki ab kami kya hai*
>
> —Mah Laqha Chanda

> (The Spring season is here, there is colour and intoxicating joy
> By the grace of God, there is no dearth of pleasure and joy)

Najma Khala's Splendid Kaleji

It was Baqreid, or Eid-us-zuha (also known as Eid-al-Adha), yesterday. At her home, Najma Khala had *qurbani ka gosht* (blessed meat offering), and she cooked some kaleji (liver). She has brought it to share with us all. We will savour it with a *degh* (large metal pot) of biryani, also made from the qurbani ka gosht, cooked at our home. Eid-us-zuha, or the 'Festival of Sacrifice', is the second of two major Muslim festivals known as Eid and celebrated in India and worldwide each year (the other being Eid-al-Fitr). It honours the willingness of Ibrahim to sacrifice his dearest possession, his first-born son Ismail, to comply with Allah's command. Just as Ibrahim was going to sacrifice his son, Allah, in his mercy, placed a lamb in his place instead. To commemorate this act of devotion, an animal such as a goat or sheep is sacrificed (known as *qurbani*) and divided into three parts: one third of the share is given to the poor and needy; another third is given to neighbours and relatives; and the remaining portion is cooked at home for the family. The division is precise and *hissas*, or small portions of the meat, are given away promptly and in accordance with the norm. It also marks the culmination of the annual religious pilgrimage to the holy city of Mecca that many Muslims across the world perform. It is an important component of Islam, and every Muslim endeavours to undertake this journey to Saudi Arabia at least once in their life.

The night before Eid, we make preparations for the day ahead. Clothes, bangles, food preparation and organizing, so much is to be done! We are given the task of chopping vast quantities of nuts, chhuarey and raisins. Several dozens of plates, bowls and spoons are taken out from the dusty recesses of a cupboard, carefully rinsed and dried, and stacked up for the guests the next day. Once we have completed our various chores, all of us girls decorate our hands in simple yet beautiful mehndi patterns—these have been painted by the women in the house and therefore lack the intricate finesse of professionals in the present day who use cones and laminated, bound catalogues of mesmerizing and complex designs. A whittled-down matchstick is dipped in a large bowl of freshly ground mehndi leaves from a bush in Amma's courtyard, with a bit of *katha*, or catechu paste, added to it. We either get a solid circle with tiny dots around it or a blob of mehndi is placed in our palm, and we make a tight fist and then open it. There is a Rorschach kind of pattern that is fascinating and unique. For the older girls, there may be a *turanj* (paisley kind of pattern), a chequered design or even floral patterns. There is fevered discussion among the cousins as to the various tricks and hacks to make the colour of the mehndi deeper and more vibrant. Don't wash your hands with soap, says one. Apply Vicks, suggests another, place your hands above a hot iron *tawa*—this one is immediately vetoed by our mother. We have varying results with all the *totke*, or tricks, and proudly show our hands to everyone. There are giggles, titters and whispers when we are told that the darker the colour of our mehndi, the more our future mother-in-law will love us!

The day begins with early morning prayers at the mosque, or more traditionally, a special open-air enclosure in many cities and towns known as *Eidgah*. The noted writer, Munshi Premchand, in his iconic story, 'Eidgah', paints a beautiful picture of one such place set in a small town in UP. It tells a heart-warming tale of a little boy named Hamid and his day at the Eidgah. It is a very touching story of how Hamid, surrounded by all the tempting sweets and treats, forgoes these to buy a pair of tongs, or *chimta*, for his beloved grandmother, as he had often seen her burn her hands while making rotis for him. He uses up his precious Eidi money for the tongs, while his friends spend theirs on colourful toys and sweets.

The special prayers are followed by a sermon, or *khutba*, by the Imam who leads the prayers and the congregation. The khutba generally extols the virtues of charity and piety and the importance of regular prayers. They may also provide guidance on prevalent social issues. Once this is over, everyone in the congregation embraces the person standing in prayer on either side, three times, as well as their own friends similarly. In smaller towns, there is usually a fair-like atmosphere as people emerge from their prayers. These festivities were an important part of the Baqreid, which we spent many times with our paternal grandparents in Pilibhit. A rickety, wooden Ferris wheel, or *hindola*, creaking under the weight of excited children dressed in their finery, is a fixture at many of these events. Festooned with sparkling strips of tinsel and colourful balloons, this is a familiar sight at these Eid melas. As little children, we too accompanied our father to the Eid prayers, dressed in our shiny new Eid clothes. There were always a few stalls selling traditional toys, like a stringed instrument made of wicker, clay and paper that somehow only the toy seller could play with a

degree of finesse with a little wicker bow. It was reminiscent of
the song 'Saiyyan jhooton ka bada sartaj nikla' from the 1957 film
Do Aankhen Barah Haath. Another toy would be a dugduggi, a
two-sided, handheld drum with a thread tied to a pebble that
struck the drum's stretched skin, making a sound. Tiny fake
birds made with brightly painted bird feathers and some tightly
wound hay, hung from a thread, and paper kites in various
colours, with their own special reinforced string, or manjha.
Hand-embellished cloth puppets shaped like parrots and cotton
wool-stuffed cloth dolls, dressed in shiny traditional outfits and
with long jet-black braids, made from scraps of knitting wool.
The miniature clay kitchen pots, or handkuliya, for little girls to
'cook' in using a bonfire kind of kindling. There were brightly
painted clay dolls too, with their heads nodding and bobbing
from side to side. The extending snake was made with equal
lengths of bamboo sticks joined in their middle and opened
like a concertina to startle others, with a devious-looking snake
head made of coloured paper. Rattles of various kinds and
simple wooden toys like spinning tops and yoyos, hollow clay
gullaks, or piggy banks, shaped like an elephant or a monkey,
brightly painted but rather fragile! And, of course, hard-boiled
sweets that you could suck for ages called kampat and bright
orange-coloured sweets, shaped like segments of a peeled orange
or lemony yellow tiny fish, or rose-pink-coloured round sweets,
goliyan, wrapped in panni, or tinsel pieces. A man would sit
by a spinning drum-like pan, magically fashioning plumes of
fluorescently bright pink candyfloss, known as budhiya ka
kata. There would be mounds of domed discs called batashey,
made of sugar and snowy white in colour. We bought them all,
devoured the sweets and hoarded the toys until they eventually
broke or fell apart.

I miss my favourite old-fashioned children's sweet that our father bought for us at Diwali, along with colourful *qandeels*, or paper lanterns, and earthenware diyas. The *shakar ke khilauney* (edible toys made from sugar) that were opaque white and hard but melted in the mouth like snowflakes. They were shaped like various recognizable animals, such as a monkey, elephant or lion, and usually had a flat base. The best thing was that the size was such that each of them used to fit perfectly in a child's palm, so one could sit for ages, happily chiselling off sweet shards with one's teeth.

Once people reach home from the Eidgah or, in some cases masjid, it is time to visit their extended families and friends to greet them. Many special dishes are prepared to welcome the guests, and there is a general atmosphere of conviviality and gaiety. Shami kebabs, biryani, dahi bade and a sweet preparation, either sewaiyyan or firni, are just some of the dishes that make up the spread. Each family has their own special snacks, dishes, ways of preparing a particular food, and their own twist on these commonly prepared dishes. Some people prefer to have more vegetarian options such as pakode, samosas, chholey, fruit chaat, halwa puri and paneer-based snacks. Some prefer a full-on meat fest, including decadently rich qormas served with sheermal, unusual kinds of kebabs, and, for the adventurous, tandoori, skewered mutton tikkas. In Amma's home and later in our mother's, kaleji is a very special and quintessentially Baqreid delicacy.

Kaleji, or liver, can be cooked along with the kidneys (gurdey-kaleji as it is known) or in a dry masala form on its own. Kaleji is certainly an acquired taste, one that I am fortunate to have acquired. The dense, boggy texture and chewiness do not appeal to all. Some find the smell off-putting. However, with

Najma Khala's version, there is no odour, just morsels of spicy
deliciousness that we have all come to love. Bite-sized pieces of
fresh liver are gently simmered in water along with cloves to
'purify' it and absolve it of all nastiness and biliousness. The
scum from the liver rises to the top, and it is carefully spooned
off. The pieces are then drained and cooked in a spicy masala
that coats them and gives them an out-of-this-world flavour. They
are sensational as a snack for visitors on Eid, on little cocktail
sticks, served with wedges of fresh lemon, but they are also
part of a proper meal, eaten with roti and sabzi. The balance of
flavours is just perfect. Nothing overpowering or askew in any
way—just an intensely delectable and pleasurable dish lovingly
made. It's just as well that she refers to each beloved child as
'mere kaleje ke tukde'!

The accompanying biryani, made at home, is just as
sensational. Perfectly spiced pieces of meat, cooked with layers
of special rice, cooked on dum and streaked with bright orange.
It is so fragrant that you can smell it even before you enter the
house, let alone the kitchen! I am sure the passers-by on foot
and in rickshaws can also savour the enticing smells. It has
been made in a degh with a snake-like winding strip of dough
sealing off the lid. The degh is another ancient relic, handed
down the generations, of generous proportions and heavy
with its copper build and a soot-blackened bottom. Sakina
has also made some lal mirch aur lassan ki chutney (a fiery,
intensely garlicky chutney made with copious amounts of raw
garlic and soaked, dried red chillies, traditionally hand-ground
on a slab of stone, using a smaller piece of triangular stone
known as sil-batta to make a paste) to accompany the biryani
and a large glass bowl of cucumber raita to conversely cool us
down. The raita is home-made curd with grated cucumber, a

pinch of rock salt and roasted cumin seed powder. Refreshing, cooling and comfortingly creamy. The garlic chutney, a perfect and harmonious accompaniment to the biryani, is so strongly pungent that the smell of garlic lingers long after the meal, resisting every remedial measure and counteraction in the form of peppermints, fennel seeds or cardamoms. But who's complaining? We are full to the bursting point. There is a pleasing sound of empty plates being cleared away and sighs of satisfaction all around us. Hands washed, we all linger around the chowki to hear more family gossip and, if we are lucky, another of Amma's fascinating *qisse* (tales).

Everyone marvels at the kaleji, which has, unsurprisingly, been polished off. Amma praises Najma Khala, and in turn, she simpers with pride and pleasure. She is very petite and bashful, and blushes at the volley of compliments directed towards her. She is delicate in build and has smooth, porcelain skin, envied by all. Her lustrous, long jet-black hair, braided thickly, reaches her waist. She wears a deep pink rose in full bloom, tucked behind her ear, and a multitude of colourful glass bangles interspersed with a few carefully chosen gold *kangan* (bracelets) on her delicate and slender arms. She is wearing a sky-blue satin gharara and has hand-embroidered her matching qameez with hundreds of tiny pearly beads to make a beautiful and artistic border on the *daaman*, or hem. The organza dupatta has *karchob bael* embroidery, running in diagonal floral, sinuously wavy lines. An exquisite hand-stitched border, or *takan*, of a serrated edging, completes the dupatta's embellishments. A dupatta without any takan or adornment is sacrilege for her! Huge, dangling, chandelier-shaped sparkling earrings cascade down from her earlobes (Amma calls this type of earrings *jhaaley*). These oscillate furiously from her stretched earlobes every time she nods and almost reach her delicate, bird-like shoulders. It is an understatement to say that she loves dressing up! She is always resplendent in well-coordinated, shiny, heavily embellished and colourful clothes, whatever the occasion, and spends her time dreaming up newer outfits and reading romantic fiction.

As everyone has overindulged in the feast today, Amma's famous and trusted home-made chuuran makes a much-needed arrival. Amma has a secret recipe in which saunf (fennel seeds), ajwain (carom seeds), kala namak (black salt), nausadar (ammonium chloride) and a few other magical ingredients are hand-ground to a powder by Sakina and stored in a jar for future use. It was initially created by her grandmother, who was known as Bilqees Dadi. Bilqees Dadi was an enthusiastic follower of traditional medicine and of the use of natural substances and plants to treat minor illnesses. She grew a multitude of medicinal herbs in a corner of her courtyard and dispensed powders, potions and *marhams* (ointments), diligently produced in tiny quantities. These were meant for just members of the household, and she was greatly respected for her knowledge and *shifaa*. The small purple and grey jar has a tight-fitting lid, which is just as well as the smell is quite overpowering. However, it does what it is meant to do, and we feel a lot more comfortable. The braver of us (or, shall we say, the more gluttonous of us) venture towards the sewaiyyan, left over from yesterday.

Sewaiyyan is a dish made with fine vermicelli, cooked with milk, khoya, sugar and chopped dried fruit, including raisins, chhuarey and nuts, that thickens to form the most delectable bowl of gorgeousness known to us. It is also flavoured with cardamom and kewra (pandanus). The resultant smell is so characteristic of Eid that the mere smell of it, even to this day, transports us to our childhood Eid celebrations. It is traditionally made at Eid, and different families have different versions of this delicacy. Some call it sheer khurma (cooked with dates), not sewaiyyan, others opt for a non-milky one, the qiwami sewain, which is cooked in chaashni or sugar syrup and ghee and is drier in consistency. A special dry sewaiyyan, made in Eastern UP uses enormous quantities of sugar, several times the amount of vermicelli used, pure ghee, makhana (lotus seeds), pistachios and saffron. It is truly decadent and gut-busting, and perhaps it is difficult for anyone to eat more than a bowlful at a time. Many have attempted and failed (me included), but the best thing (apart from the incredible taste) is that because of all that sugar, it lasts forever. It is almost like jam made out of delicate vermicelli strands! On a serious note, there are many regional variations and subtle differences in sewaiyyan made in the Indian subcontinent; another version that is made in Hyderabad even uses meat.

These are usually made in a large *donga* (tureen) and served in tiny cut-glass or delicate porcelain bowls. Amma's favourite donga is one of the few remaining pieces from an old dinner set dating back to her mother's wedding. It is creamy white porcelain and has large pink and orange flowers all around the outer surface. The bottom of the donga is chipped in some places from many years of use, and a delicate grey spider's web-like pattern has formed on it. It is still perfectly usable, though! There are extended horizontal edges from the rim on either side, which make it easy to hold and carry the somewhat heavy donga, and we are always thankful when we make it to the table with the donga intact. Amma has great anecdotes about some of the crockery she owns. A lot of it goes back to *angrezon ka zamana* (the British Raj), and these fine porcelain items were probably made in England and were used in Amma's home. Some tea sets and dinner sets were part of her wedding gifts, and some heirloom pieces had been passed down through the generations, including a large Moradabadi ladle.

Every now and then, these metal items are sent for *qalai*, and they come back gleaming. The qalaiwala comes home every few months to ask if any of the pots, pans or platters need to be polished. A few assorted *taamba* (copper) items such as *rakabiyan* (dishes), *badiya* (bowls) *kafgeer* (ladle), a *seeni* (platter or a large tray), *sarposh* (a metal cloche or domed cover for dishes), a *paandan* (a metal box for storing fresh paan and its various components), a *degh*, *khassdan* (an ornate domed container for keeping paan) and a few smaller *katorey* (metal bowls for drinking water in) are given to this man. He sits cross-legged on the passage just outside the courtyard in a corner and plies his trade, rubbing the pots furiously with rags soaked in a wide array of chemicals and then rinsing them off. We would sometimes hover and watch him plying his trade. The sizzling sounds, the acrid smoke, the swirling potions and the makeshift fire with its flames licking the item, almost seem magical. The objects are now gleaming and blemish-free, as if new. Except that they are not. Amma is delighted with the treasure trove beside her and gazes lovingly at the various items, reminiscing about the days gone by and memories of her youth. The sheen and brilliance of these reflect her own self, and she can trace her entire life's joys and sorrows in the subtle markings and grooves of these much-loved objects of daily use.

Coming back to the Eid feast, it is memorable in many aspects and will continue to be the benchmark for many Eids to come. Even today, when we celebrate Eid in far-flung lands without the gaiety and *raunaq* (brightness) that were part of these celebrations with a large extended family, the memories fill our hearts with pleasure and nostalgia, like coming across a beautiful flower, picked long, long ago and pressed in an old, dog-eared, much-loved book.

Kaleji

500 gm fresh mutton kaleji, rinsed well
½ tsp red chilli powder
3–4 whole cloves
½ tsp roasted cumin powder
1 medium onion, finely chopped
1 tbsp ginger-garlic paste
1 fresh green chilli, finely chopped
1 tbsp fenugreek seeds
½ tsp turmeric powder
½ tsp coriander powder
2 tbsp cooking oil
salt to taste
2 tbsp curd or plain yoghurt

For the garnish:
a pinch of garam masala
lemon wedges
fresh coriander sprigs

Wash the pieces of liver thoroughly and drain.

Gently simmer the liver pieces along with the whole cloves in a pot half filled with boiling water.

As the scum rises, remove it carefully with a spoon and set aside the liver pieces. Discard the cloves and cooking water.

In a *karahi*, or wok, heat the oil and add the fenugreek seeds. Take care that these do not turn black, or else the nutty taste of these turns bitter.

In a couple of seconds, add the chopped onion and sauté until it turns golden brown.

Add the ginger-garlic paste, green chillies, turmeric, coriander, cumin and red chilli powders. Add salt as per your taste.

Gently cook them down, adding a splash of water if needed. Stir continuously, on a low to medium heat until a thick paste is formed with little patches of oil separating.

Add the boiled liver and mix together.

Beat the curd in a small bowl until smooth and devoid of lumps, and add it to the pot.

Cook again for 5–6 minutes. The gravy at the end should be dry and stick to the pieces of liver, coating them fully.

Serve on a platter with a sprinkle of garam masala and finely chopped coriander leaves. Place a few wedges of lemon at the edges. Place cocktail sticks alongside to spear each divine morsel.

Another popular dish made on special occasions, such as Eid, are these tiny morsels of exquisite flavour and texture. These are different from the more common shami kebab, which uses cooked qeema ground down to a paste. This adventurous and rather dramatic version uses raw mince, imbued with many exciting flavours of roasted spices and a very enticing deep smoky flavour. Once eaten, they are never forgotten. They are either served as a snack on their own or with a fresh mint and coriander chutney to offset the pungent smokiness and piquant taste. Alternatively, they can be part of a main meal or daawat too, served with saalan and roti or a robust biryani or pulao at a dinner gathering. Najma Khala's recipe is as follows:

Kacchey Qeeme ke Kebab

Makes about 8

250 gm fine, lean mutton mince
1 tsp raw papaya paste
salt to taste
2 onions, finely chopped
1 tsp ginger-garlic paste
½ tsp garam masala
½ tsp red chilli powder

A roasted and powdered special masala mix for this:
½ tsp poppy seeds
2 almonds
½ tsp desiccated coconut
½ tsp fennel seeds
½ tsp coriander seeds
2 tsp besan

For dhungaar (smokiness):
a clean onion skin
a small piece of coal ember
½ tsp ghee or a knob of butter

First add the qeema, raw papaya paste and salt to a bowl. Mix well, cover and leave to marinate for 2 hours.

In a heavy-bottomed vessel, gently brown the onions to caramelize fully and get a nice brown colour and a characteristic smell. It takes time, so be patient. Add the ginger-garlic paste and chilli powder and stir a few times on low heat.

Let it cool. Transfer to a large bowl or deep dish.

Add the garam masala, the special mix and the marinated qeema and incorporate them all.

Make a little well in the centre, using a spoon. In this cavity, place a clean onion skin with the butter or ghee within it. Place the hot coal ember with a pair of tongs and cover immediately with a lid or plate. Keep it covered for 2 minutes. Discard the ember and onion skin remnants carefully and safely. A deep and intense smoky flavour would have permeated the qeema.

Make small, flattened patties by rolling the qeema gently between your palms. Shallow fry in hot oil on a low heat to ensure they are cooked through.

Serve on a platter with fine rings of onion and wedges of lemon, if desired.

~

Eid, or for that matter, festivities of any kind, bring forth memories and shared memories of our ancestors. These provide a link to our pasts and allow these wonderful people to live on forever in our hearts. The saddest thing is when one stops talking about people who have passed on. The obliteration of the memory of these people seems to remove every last shadow of their existence. After a few generations, it is as if they were never there. So it is vitally important that we continue to remember them, whether it is by making a dish they used to make, wearing an item of jewellery that belonged to them or even reading their favourite poetry.

Sab kahaan kuch lala-o-gul mein numayan ho gayin
Khaak mein kya suratein hongi ki pinhaan ho gayin

—Mirza Ghalib

(Some, not all manifested themselves as beautiful flowers
What faces would have been hidden in the dust)

Rana Momani's Suji Halwa Squares

It is Shab-e-Baraat, or the night of forgiveness. A night in the month of Shaban, as per the Islamic calendar, which many Muslims revere as the night of seeking forgiveness and mercy and pray through the night, asking Allah (SWT) to bless them. Believers stay up all night and offer prayers seeking clemency for any sins committed knowingly or unwittingly in the past.

Amma wants to have large quantities of halwa made at home so portions of it can be sent to neighbours and members of the extended family who live close by. A soft, sweet and rich suji ka halwa (semolina halwa) is made, which has been served on beautifully patterned little china plates, each covered with a hand-embroidered cloth napkin, and placed on trays. Of course, the napkins are repurposed from an old plain cotton bedsheet, painstakingly cut in neat squares, with a hand-crocheted lace edging, and with a beautiful and dainty basket of flowers embroidered on it with *resham* (a special embroidery thread with several skeins and in many different colours and a subtle sheen to it). The old bed sheet had unfortunately been burned in one corner by the overzealous *dhobi* and his extra hot iron, and he had duly been admonished. Amma wouldn't dream of throwing the lovely cambric cloth away, and thus these exquisite cloth napkins came into being. A small portion of the home-made halwa is reserved for *niyaz*, which is the ritual of blessing food by reading special verses from the Holy Quran over it. It is important that until the niyaz is done, no halwa is eaten, even to taste it, so it remains pure. We patiently wait for this to happen and hover eagerly. The hot suji ka halwa, made with asli ghee, sugar, cardamoms, raisins and chopped nuts, and sprinkled with desiccated coconut, smells heavenly. The aroma of suji being gently roasted in pan over a low heat fills the kitchen and permeates through to the aangan. It is a nutty, earthy and comforting smell. We have been asked to wash our hands and chop the dried fruit and nuts finely and precisely. The slivers of blanched almonds for decoration are kept aside for the final flourish. The niyaz will be done on a small portion of the halwa, along with water in one of Amma's *katorey*, or bowls used for drinking.

After a while, Rana Momani arrives. She brings with her the same plate that she was sent the halwa on and it is covered with Amma's napkin. She affectionately hugs Amma and then all of us. She lives close by and has brought some of the halwa that she made at home, for us. People prepare different varieties of halwa on this auspicious occasion. Some use besan (chickpea flour), others moong ki dal or chaney ki dal, but the one with suji is most traditionally made in homes. Halwas are generally made with grains, like semolina, derived from wheat, or pulses and also with vegetables like carrots, bottle gourd (lauki) or pumpkin, but the most decadent halwa is, of course, andey ka halwa, or a halwa made with eggs. With great quantities of ghee, sugar and nuts, this is certainly not for the faint-hearted or the calorie-conscious! The taste is magnificent, though, and it is made as a special treat, warming and comforting in the bone-chilling winter months. The unctuous richness of the eggs, cooked gently and with great care, imparts a flavour and robustness that are exceptional. If that were not enough, an even more rich and luxurious version uses just the egg yolks rather than whole eggs for a deep golden colour and greater intensity of flavour and sumptuousness Of course, some halwas were too elaborate to be cooked at home. Sohan Halwa, a Rampur specialty was one such delightful and sinfully rich treat. It is made with samnak, or germinated wheat flour, and has a chewy, slightly granular, fudge-like texture. It was always a special occasion when a box of this came. Karachi halwa was another such offering, jelly-like and vividly coloured, with a split kaju (cashew) stuck on it.

Rana Momani is not one of the cousins in the clan but is married to one. Her husband, Tariq Mamu, is one of Mummy's younger cousins, her khala's son. So even though she is an outsider, we have known her for many years. She is affectionate and warm, and has won over the hearts of even the harder-to-please members of the extended family. She is soft-spoken, polite and a very gracious host. Whenever we visit her, she always has some home-made treats for us.

The suji ka halwa Rana Momani has prepared is the brittle variety and is cut in the shape of diamonds. She calls them *qatliyan*. The pieces are artfully piled up on the plate and studded with slivers of almond and chopped pistachio. Each *qatli* is perfectly and evenly cut, as if with a geometry ruler—an edible rhombus, if you like! The rigid pieces have a bite, like a biscuit, and once bitten, they melt in the mouth into a sweet, crumbly mouthful of pure pleasure. She is an excellent and innovative cook and experiments with different kinds of halwa each year, be it anjeer (fig) or adrak (ginger), khubani (dried apricots) or khajoor (dates) but has settled for this more traditional one this year. She carefully folds Amma's napkin away and places the plate of qatlis on the chowki. Sakina brings tea, and we all enjoy a piece or two.

Many years later, I will look back and never cease to be amazed at the resourcefulness, creativity and gumption of the women in the family. They know the art of 'creating something out of nothing'. In an almost magical way, conjuring up veritable feasts at the drop of a hat, creating perfectly satisfying meals if an unexpected visitor turns up, and prudently using something that is ordinary, plentiful and seasonal and turning it into something beautiful and exceptional. Anyone who was fortunate to visit their homes never went back hungry. Not ones to automatically rip open a packet of biscuits or packaged snacks, they made sure all visitors had at the very least a nice cup of freshly made tea or, in hot weather, home-made sharbat like lemonade, phalse ka sharbat, bel ka sharbat, chhach or aam pana. Along with this would be some home-made snacks, using whatever they happened to have at home at the time. Some treats were made in large batches and stored for unexpected visitors. These wholesome goodies, devoid of artificial colours, flavours and preservatives were offered to guests with pride and the wonderful concept that is *barkat*. The satisfaction of feeding someone well, to the best of your resources, and sharing the abundance and blessings with not just family but everyone around oneself is what defines the word barkat. It is a boon from the Almighty, a blessing that has given us the wherewithal to not just buy but also to appreciate and utilize the *rizq* we have been granted. Rizq is an all-encompassing word for goodness and beneficial things in our lives, such as faith, food, health, family and prosperity.

It was also about making do with what was at hand rather than rushing to shops with a list of ingredients, as is the norm now if one wishes to make a celebratory, special dish. Which is why it was frustrating and futile to ask Amma or any of the other aunts and relatives to give precise measurements for ingredients. When it came to special items such as nuts or dry fruit, the stock response was '*tumhare paas jitna ho, dal do* (as much as you can add)'. Therefore, there were countless variations of the same dish, each amazing and fabulous in its own right. Of course, these ladies also possessed that magic touch that transforms an ordinary dish into something spectacular and perfect. It is called haath ka maza, or the special skill of the person creating that dish, a result of many years of practice, patience and attention to detail. These are my true food heroes.

It was common to make namak parey, shakar parey, sev and other such chai-accompanying snacks in large batches and store them in reused jars, tins and *martbans*. One wintertime snack that Amma often made was pittauway, with bajra flour, jaggery and ghee. These were mixed together and formed into a rough dough, then flattened by hand into small discs and deep-fried. These were great with a steaming cup of tea. She also made something called khajoor, which, although it is the Urdu word for dates, has absolutely nothing to do with them. A simple sweet dough was made with atta (flour), a lot of home-made khaalis, pure ghee, sugar and a pinch of crushed cardamom seeds. This was then spread thinly like roti dough across a bamboo winnowing fan, a lightweight handheld platter-like implement (used to thresh gehun or wheat grain) that was called *soop*. The striated, woven texture of the soop imprinted itself on the dough, giving it an interesting pattern similar to the irregularly undulating, ragged exterior of dates. This was then painstakingly cut into diamond-shaped pieces, the size of biscuits and deep fried in oil. We found the name soop rather mystifying as it sounded like western soup but was nothing like it and wasn't even slurp-worthy or edible! Amma, with her characteristic humour and wisdom, responded with one of her many *kahawats*: '*Soop boley toh boley, chhalni kya boley, usmein toh bahattar chhed hain!* (A person who is flawless can speak; others with shortcomings should remain silent)'. The soop is now not a thing to be mocked but rather a useful, steadfast implement that has made an impression on our young minds (and as we have seen, it is rather good at making an impression!) We often see rural women standing in crop fields as we travel by car to and from Aligarh, holding aloft a larger version of the soop, patiently separating grain from chaff.

Amma has a saying for every occasion and descriptive terms for people. We find that very amusing, and Amma patiently explains them to us. Her everyday spoken language is peppered with these, and it seems like an exciting code-language specific to our family—very thrilling for our young minds! One of our favourites is for someone who shows unwarranted excessive familiarity in order to ingratiate themselves or seek a favour: *Jaan na pehchaan, badhi khala salaam!* It has us in splits, as does: *Main kahoon mera kamarband suney*, for a very meek, soft-spoken person. A sulky, brooding type of person was a *ghunna*, and someone with an unwashed face, usually a child, was a *billi munh chaata* (literally a cat-licked face). A two-faced person, *adha teetar adha bater*, a very distant relative, a *mamu tamu ke tamtayya*, an unlikely bit of gossip, or fake news as it is called these days, *chandukhaney ki khabar*. A very tall woman would be dubbed a *Paharh Khan* (literally mountain-like), especially when married to a tiny, wiry man, a *piddhi*. *Chaney mein matar milaana* was to intrude on a private conversation; a badly dressed woman was a *fatthoh faqirni*; *ghodhey daurana* was to pull a few strings to get an important job done; *phir wahi dho dho geela*, for a person who rues about their own past failures and misfortunes endlessly; *huqqa pani bundh* meant all privileges were taken away. Other phrases she frequently used were: *jal bhun ke khaak* (an excessively jealous person) and *taapte reh gaye* (was left hopping mad) for a person wringing his hands in frustration. A deserted place or a poorly attended function was one where *kaana kauwa bhi nahi tha* (not even a one-eyed crow attended), a *pilpila aam*, was used for an ineffectual person in an important post, *sab din changey, tyohar ke din nangey* (one who dresses well everyday but fails to make an effort on special occasions), which makes us giggle no end, as did her admonishing a teen still in their pyjamas at noon with *kapde badlo, aadmi bano; kya fatthoh faqirni bani phir rahi ho* (which was a very peculiar command for us girls!); *udhey udhey phirna* (for a self-important haughty person); also *aap hi aap mein dabal*. She had no time for superficial, fake people and could spot them from a mile away.

A favourite saying of hers is: *Khao man chaha, pehno jag chaha* (Eat as you like, wear what the world likes).

On the topic of food, she used another phrase when someone who was feeling less than energetic and enthusiastic about a task had been fed. They promptly became full of verve and very compliant:

Peyt mein parha daana, matakney laga kaana

(Literally, the one-eyed person began to dance once fed)

Amma, though not overly religious, was deeply spiritual and a believer in certain Islamic rituals, such as niyaz. Usually, a halwa of some sort would be made, pure and untouched while cooking to maintain its *paak* status (purity). Once a prayer had been said, we all received a small portion in our clean, cupped hands, briefly bringing them to our foreheads, taking care not to spill anything, before eating it respectfully. Apart from niyaz to mark the birthdate of family members, before the start of anything auspicious or important such as a wedding, success in higher education or a safe return from an arduous journey, and of course on Eid, Amma also followed a few other special niyaz rituals. Such as *Ghaus Pak ki Niyaz*, to honour Sheikh Abdul Qadir Jeelani. A special rice preparation known as tosha was made with sugar, rice and ghee. Tosha is similar to zarda pulao but devoid of the characteristic vibrant yellow colour and embellishments, such as the coloured pieces of candied fruit peel that are sometimes added to zarda to make it look even more festive and enticing. The austere and pale appearance of the offering perhaps emphasized its purity of purpose further. It could be done as part of a *Ghusl-e-sehat*, a celebratory meal held in gratitude for one who has recovered from a serious illness or healed after a life-threatening physical injury or mishap.

Ashra, which falls on the tenth day of the month of Moharram, the first month of the Islamic calendar, marks the day on which the battle of Karbala took place. It was a tragic day that resulted in the martyrdom of Husain, the grandson of Prophet Muhammad. Sometimes, we are invited to meetings of mourning, known as majlis, and hear heart-rending, painful accounts and lamentations in remembrance of the tragic events. We hear soulful and deeply sad poetic recitations known as *marsiya*, *soz* and *noha*. It is difficult to listen to these and not shed a tear, as they are powerful and use highly emotive words. Devoid of music, in a gathering clad in plain, unadorned black clothes, the suffering and hardships faced are retold in stirring, heart-rending laments.*

In Amma's home, and later in our mother's home, khichda was made to mark this occasion.

Another special and unique niyaz that a few women from Amma's circle of friends and extended family performed was *koondey*. We have been invited to a few and are familiar with the sweet, puri-like offerings in special earthenware bowls known as koondey. We know that we must approach the table where they are laid out and eat them respectfully, with our heads covered, and with great care and with humility. This is to honour Imam Jaafar Sadiq, an ancient Islamic *aalim*, or learned man. It is held in the month of Rajab. These activities of faith have more cultural and social value than purely religious ones and the etiquette and belief, or *aqeeda*, in them are vital to the performance of the rituals. Any disrespect, or *be-adbi*, is to be avoided at all costs, be it in preparation or partaking of the blessed foods. A special niyaz, such as this usually follows the fulfilment of a *mannat*, or asking a special favour, be it the fixing of a marriage, a good job or recovery from a serious illness.

In our homes, till today, an *imam-zaamin* (amulet) is always tied to the upper right arm of a person before they embark on a journey. Hand-stitched from scraps of fabric material, with a small amount of money sewn inside it, it is taken off when the traveller returns home safely. The amulet is opened, and a niyaz is done on some mithai purchased with the money and given to the poor as a prayer of thanks for the safe arrival. Among Shia Muslims, according to historian Rana Safvi, the engagement ceremony is called *Iman zamin ki rasam*, and specially made ornate ones are tied on the arm of a Shia bride. The tradition has its origin in Imam

---

* Rakhshanda Jalil, literary historian. Taken with permission from her writings.

Raza, the eighth Shia Imam, who, during the rule of Mamun-al Rashid, was considered the guarantor of safe journeys.

A special prayer, or *fateha*, is done for a member of a family who has departed, as is a Quran Khwani (a recitation of the entire holy book, the thirty chapters, or *siparey*, done by a group of readers). Often to commemorate the death anniversary of a family member who has departed, small children from the local madrasa or masjid are invited to read a few chapters each and are later given food and sharbat. The practice of a large number of people gathering to complete a reading of the Quran is called *baqshna*, ensuring the departed person's passage to the other side is peaceful. This also protects them from the *qabr ke azaab*, or horrors of the grave, soon after death. Amma also tells us about acts of piety and kindness that constitute *sawab*. These could include education of the underprivileged, charitable acts, providing clean drinking water in hot weather, providing shelter for the homeless, planting trees, helping the elderly cross a road or reading to them, and helping orphanages with books and food. She instils in us the importance of these simple acts of kindness.

Amma is also a believer in *peers* (holy men) and *dargahs* (exalted shrines or tombs), but to a lesser degree. She has a deep respect for these, but we have perhaps been to only a handful of these with her. We all know the well-known dargahs of Hazrat Khwaja Moinuddin Chishti at Ajmer, Hazrat Khwaja Nizamuddin Auliya, a stone's throw from our own home in Delhi, and Shaikh Saleem Chishti at Fatehpur Sikri, to name a few. When we visited her in Kashmir, we also visited the Hazratbal Dargah in Srinagar, right outside the Kashmir University campus. A beautiful marbled, domed structure, it is tranquil and calming. The Dal Lake is close by, and it is an aesthetically beautiful place to visit and pay our respects. Abba had established the Iqbal Institute in the Urdu department of the University and was its chairman. We spent many idyllic summer holidays savouring the ethereal beauty and rich culture of Kashmir. Those days will forever remain in my heart as a beautiful reminder of a truly special place. Some friends of Amma took us to the dargah at Anantnag, also in Kashmir, a stunning and other-worldly location with the clear mountain air and beautiful flowers surrounding it. There is an indescribable atmosphere of enchantment and mysticism.

A lesser-known one at Kalliyar Sharif, near Saharanpur, is dear to Amma's heart, as her father donated an ornate silver-plated wooden gate to the dargah. His name is still painted on the board on the wall, written in beautifully scripted Nastaleeq Urdu lettering. We visit it and find it peaceful and tranquil, unlike the more popular ones with throngs of believers, beggars and hawkers, all jostling for space and money.

We listen to the Sufi qawwalis at the dargahs we visit with great respect and fascination. We've been to several live renditions of traditional qawwals and find them moving and spellbinding.

Amir Khusro's haunting and deeply poetic words, in particular, though simple, create such masterful drama and atmosphere, and we are magically transported to a realm beyond reality.

> *Chhaap tilak sab chheeni re mosey naina milaikey . . .*
> *. . . gori gori baiyyan hari hari choorhiyan*
> *Bayyan pakarh dhar leeni ray mosey naina milaike*

> (You robbed me of myself, my persona, with a mere glance
> My fair arms, adorned with green bangles
> You held me captive, with a mere glance)

Later in the day, more halwa arrives from other homes. We are spoiled for choice! We sample each and then have an animated discussion among us about the good and bad points of each and rate them accordingly.

Rana Momani's qatliyon wala halwa wins unanimously.

Qatliyon Wala Suji ka Halwa

Though fairly simple to make, it requires a degree of patience and planning to turn out perfectly. As the hot halwa sets quickly, it is useful to grease a clean, dry thali with a bit of ghee or oil before starting to make the halwa. This ensures easy removal of the pieces once they have set. Chop the nuts prior to cooking the halwa and keep them aside.

2 cups suji (semolina)
1 cup sugar
1 cup water
2–3 cardamom seeds, finely crushed
1/2 cup ghee

For the garnish:
almond flakes and chopped pistachios
2 tbsp desiccated coconut

Grease a thali with ghee or oil and sprinkle with some of the chopped nuts. Keep this and the remaining nuts aside.

Prepare the syrup by adding the sugar, water and finely crushed cardamom seeds to a heavy-bottomed pan and cooking on a low-medium heat, stirring often. Once the sugar has dissolved and the mixture turns bubbly, turn the heat further down to a simmer and stir until the chashni, or syrup, is slightly thick and takes a while to drop from the spoon, known as a *lambi chheent* (a long drop). Keep the syrup aside.

Roast the suji in another pan. Keep stirring on a low heat until an earthy aroma arises and it turns very slightly darker. Aim for a golden-brown colour, stirring continuously for uniformity and taking care that it does not burn or catch.

Add the ghee, stir continuously with a long wooden spoon, and add the syrup. Let it cook for a while till it thickens and comes together as a soft mass. Take the pan off the heat and immediately pour the halwa over the prepared greased thali, shaking slightly to cover the dish or thali evenly.

Sprinkle with desiccated coconut and the remaining chopped nuts.

Quickly, before it sets, use a sharp knife to make transverse lines roughly equally apart, and then turn the thali further at an angle and make crossing parallel lines over the previous ones to get slightly elongated diamond shapes.

Leave for 1–2 hours to set fully, and with the knife, go over the lines deeply again. Leave for another 10 minutes or so, and then carefully prise out the pieces one by one. They will be brittle and have a bite, but will not be hard.

Carefully arrange them on a plate to serve. They can also be stored for a few days in an airtight tin or box.

One of the more richly decadent and delectable types of halwa is the famed andey ka halwa. Not one for weight-watchers or those with frugal tastes, this is a dulcet, heavenly and warming bowl of pure happiness. One that can act as a comforting hug on a dreary winter day, banishing the blues and sending shards of gentle heat and joy into the most embittered and grim corners of one's mind and heart.

It is made often in our house, especially if guests are expected for tea in the winter months or at dinner parties.

In Amma's time, an even richer version of this was made using only the egg yolks. I've never tasted that version, but I love andey ka halwa just as it is.

Andey ka Halwa

2 eggs, well beaten
1 cup full fat milk or 2 tbsp of fresh cream
1 tsp asli ghee
1 tsp desiccated coconut, plus extra for garnish
2 cardamom seeds, crushed
1 cup sugar
100 gm khoya (dried whole milk)
2 tsp besan (chickpea flour), lightly roasted on a tawa
a few drops of kewra (pandanus)

For the garnish:
slivers of blanched almonds
chopped raisins and cashews

Mix the eggs, milk or cream and ghee and add them to a heavy-bottomed pan.

Cook on a very gentle heat, stirring all the time.

When the mixture starts to turn a bit granular, add the sugar, crushed cardamom seeds and desiccated coconut.

Crumble in the khoya and add the roasted besan, stirring gently and letting it all cook through. This requires patience and a fair bit of time, but the result is absolutely worth it.

Cook until the oil starts to separate.

Add a few drops of kewra, mixing it gently through.

At this stage, the halwa looks pale beige with specks of brown and has lost the eggy smell.

Place in a serving dish and garnish with chopped nuts and raisins and a sprinkling of desiccated coconut.

~

Sulaima Chachi, a much loved and regarded relative, who is married to Abba's cousin Wali Baqsh Qadri, an eminent educationist, also makes an unusual halwa. She saves the balai (cream off the top of milk) over a few days. Then she places it with soaked chana dal in a pressure cooker to cook it through. Once cooked, the cream releases its fat, the ghee that is used to *bhuno* (gently brown) the halwa. Then she adds sugar, raisins and chopped nuts. It tastes heavenly.

Her warmth, humour and kindness endear her to us greatly and we visit her often.

Ours is a culturally Muslim family. The special rituals, supplications and practices mean a lot to us and keep the fabric of our lives from fraying and fading. It keeps our *imaan*, our sense of togetherness, and organizes our lives with the little reminders that define our family annual calendars. Our earnest duas, our pleas and our innermost wishes—perhaps the ones that we ourselves are not aware of—are our way of connecting with Allah on a personal level. We learned these as children, and many years later, we would teach them to our own children.

Nanno's Maash ki Dal

Nanno is Amma's younger sister, whom she affectionately calls Chhutto (little one). Mummy calls her Khalajan, and we call her Nanno. True to her name, she is petite and delicate in build and very sweet. She loves to embroider and makes elaborate hand-embroidered gifts for everyone. When she was younger, she would embroider tablecloths, or *mezposh*, with scalloped edges, or *kangoorey*, fabric covers for glasses and water jugs, hand crocheted and the edges weighed down with beads or even individual uncooked chaney ki dal wrapped in *gota* (tinsel ribbon) to resemble tiny golden nuggets, and of course the most gorgeous net, or *jaali*, dupattas. My mother's dolls, as a child, had an enviable wardrobe of shimmering outfits, thanks to her efficient use of scraps of silk, brocade and satin, with matching accessories. She also famously hand-stitched her own daughter-in-law's *suhag puda* by meticulously cutting and joining scraps of silk to make a kind of wrapping sheet, with sequins, beads and gota to create a stunning work of art, just to be used as packaging! Nanno loves to read novels, magazines and poetry, in Urdu, of course. She eagerly devours any publication she can lay her hands on and is well aware of current social and national issues. Unlike Amma, she is more of a homebody, preferring to stay home and read rather than dress up to go out or entertain guests for that matter! She only ever wears hand-stitched, plain white cotton ghararas, a loose white kurti and a crinkled plain white mulmul dupatta, devoid of any embellishments. Her prematurely snowy white hair is loosely backcombed and tied in a wispy braid. Soft-spoken, warm and always dressed in white, she seems quite angelic to our young minds. A pair of exceedingly thick-lensed, maroon-rimmed glasses is always perched at the tip of her tiny nose as she peers closely at the person speaking to her. A defunct, forlorn-looking cable wire from a hearing aid hangs listlessly from her hair, trailing down to her shoulders like a wilted chameli *gajra* (a hair adornment of flowers strung together). She doesn't like using it because she can't stand the *shoon-shoon* noise it makes! She wears no jewellery, not even a locket. For someone who has created such magnificent, colourful and intricate works of embroidery, her own appearance is oddly austere. Her lifelong passion is her love of Urdu poetry, in particular the poet Mir Taqi Mir. She knows all his poetry by heart and has hand-embroidered her favourite sher on her pillowcase, a nod to her quiet sense of humour and love for the poet:

Jo is shor se Mir rota rahega
To humsaya kaahe ko sota rahega

(Mir weeps so loudly
how can the neighbour/companion sleep)

As long as she was alive, a visit to Aligarh seemed incomplete without visiting her. Soon after reaching the city, we would go over to say 'Salaam' to her. She would greet us with great warmth and hold the hand of one of us girls, making us sit next to her, whispering murmured *duaein* (blessings).

One of our other favourite things to do as a family is to visit the famous Numaish, which is a much-awaited Aligarh tradition like none other. It is held in January, extending into February. It has its origins in a horse display or show for the nawab families. Later, it became a fairground for the people of Aligarh, with illuminated grounds, stalls of various kinds and lively music. It is like a fun fair, and the people of Aligarh as well as those with links to the city eagerly look forward to it.

~

We throng to the Numaish, excitedly in several rickshaws. At the gate, there is an array of fluorescent, flashing lights and announcements on the loudspeaker in chaste Urdu. We gingerly enter the arena, or the Numaish grounds. There are stalls selling *surma* (kohl), itr, glass bangles and a plethora of female adornments. These are from various places in UP that are famous for producing these items. Special handicrafts and embroidered household items are also on display. Beautiful and delicately embroidered Lucknowi Chikankari kurtas and dupattas, karchob material from Marhera and Banarsi brocade beckon and dazzle the eyes. There is pottery from Khurja, with its distinctive royal blue or ochre-coloured floral patterns on its glazed surface. We always end up buying mugs, flower vases, plates and decorative bowls, whether we need them or not! There are colourful woven mats, including prayer mats or *janamaz*, prayer caps or *topi* (the usual crocheted skull caps in white or cream, or the more extravagant velvet Rampuri ones in deep jewel colours) and woven wicker baskets from eastern UP.

There are old-fashioned wooden toys and tiny glass animals, individually hand-blown and in bright colours, from Agra. We always buy a menagerie of these delicate, very detailed glass objects, including lime green parrots with scarlet beaks, tawny lions, milky white cows, powdery blue pigeons and nut-brown monkeys, nestled together in a small cardboard box lined with unbleached cotton wool. There are stalls of furniture, including wicker chairs and wooden tables with inlay work. There are vast varieties of bed linen, including embroidered bedspreads with *patti ka kaam*, a sort of applique work, frilly pastel-coloured pillowcases and of course the famous buttery yellow and soft *mau ki chaadar*, a sort of light sheet or covering for sleeping in the warmer months. They were very comfortable, single-layered sheets, more useful against a light dawn breeze when sleeping in the open courtyard or rooftop on *niwarh ke palang*, which is a simple wooden bed frame with an off-white, wide and thick band of robust cotton fabric called *niwarh* that was woven across it. Over time, the bed would start to sag a bit and be duly tightened. I loved the saggy stage of the beds, as it felt like a hammock and had a cocooning effect.

Lotas are jug-like vessels with a spout that are essential for ablutions for Muslims. They hang in bunches from a stall's awning in various shapes, sizes, colours and materials, like a multi-headed hydra with spouts pointing in all directions. There are bright-hued basic plastic ones, squat and plump-bottomed, with a hollow plastic handle and a curved but stiff spout; graceful tall plastic ones resembling a samovar; shiny aluminium ones and elaborate Moradabadi ones, looking like something out of a set of a filmi royal court. An exchange between two AMU students is part of the folklore that defines humour, wit and, of course, the essential place of the lota. This was ostensibly asked by one student packing his belongings to go home from the hostel, and the line was, '*Wuzu ke liye lota shamil-e-safar hai na?*' To which the other student vigorously nods and replies, '*beshak*'.

We espy a stall selling a plethora of pickles. We eagerly throng towards it. Smells of spices marinating in mustard oil and a pungent, savoury aroma await us. There are traditional pickles that have brought joy to many a simple meal of dal, roti, sabzi and chawal in the villages, towns and cities all across UP for years and years. Some, such as mango, lime and chillies, are familiar, and some are enticingly new for us. We see little round greenish berries resembling green olives; the lasode ka achar, batons of carrot or radishes (mooli); plump cloves of garlic; stuffed large red chillies oozing with a fiery, spicy paste; strips of young Ramkela mango, or kairi; juliennes of ginger in vinegar and the ubiquitous mixed vegetable pickle. We buy a few jars of the red chilli pickle, licking our lips in anticipation of wolfing it down with flaky hot parathas later on at home, and mummy buys the ginger juliennes to garnish chhole and dal or to gift to friends. There are also jars of murabbas, especially amla (Indian gooseberry), and various kinds of gulqand (a kind of rose jam). Pickling and preserving are ancient ways of saving foodstuffs, especially vegetables, so that they can be enjoyed throughout the year. An inexpensive and delicious way to make food stay edible for longer and use it like a relish, however simple and sparse a meal may be.

We move from one stall to the next en masse, stopping to examine, haggle and buy whatever catches our fancy. There is a great deal of background noise, with songs blaring on the loudspeaker interspersed with advertisement jingles that we do not hear on regular radio. A shop that sells sarees and dress material, Sari Suhag, and a tonic that claims to make the mind sharper, appropriately called Dimagheen, are just some of the local businesses that air their promotional campaigns. We then make a beeline for the much-awaited and distinctive food of the Numaish. Apart from the unique and decadent halwa paratha, which we avoid as the parathas are large and greasy, we are all madly in love with the offerings of the food enclosures, known as Nazeer Hotel and Jhanda Hotel. These lofty-sounding names belie the makeshift, curtained off booths made with wooden chairs and tables. But look past the greasy glasses and chipped plates, and there is a heavenly, almost regal feast to be had. Succulent and intensely delectable seekh kebabs, freshly made and disengaged from the red-hot skewers, still flecked with embers, a chicken qorma of some sort, and hot-off-the-tawa rumali roti to scoop up the rich gravy and gosht. We throw caution to the wind and dig in, using our hands to plough through the meal quickly before the cold winter air congeals the food on our plates.

We savour and enjoy the food, laughing at old anecdotes from visits to Numaish in the years gone by. We are told, perhaps in jest, that it is customary to wipe one's hands with the curtains to fully show our appreciation, but we politely desist and rinse our hands on the ground beneath us. Sated and in a state of bliss, we venture out. Much to our delight, a brightly lit stall of digestive powders and pills, known collectively as chuuran, awaits us. We sample a few: there is an adrak (ginger) one with strips of stem ginger coated in a pungent powder mix; hingoli with asafoetida inside tiny pellets; anardana with dried pomegranate seeds, each promising quick and effective relief from indigestion. We, of course, buy copious amounts of bottles just to eat when we feel like it rather than for medicinal purposes. This is one of the highlights for us, and we never let an opportunity pass to stock up on these and sample exciting new ones. A strongly sulphurous cloud cloaks the vicinity of this stall, and we happily lick the samples from our palms and walk away with our haul.

There are stalls selling a sweet and rich breakfast item called khajela or khaja, which some people have with milk, but we have never been adventurous enough to try it. It looks like a crispy, vermicelli-like, deep-fried round disc that hangs in bunches at the stalls. We have not seen them anywhere else. There are the usual stalls of luscious pethe ki mithai from Agra, light and buttery nankhatai from Meerut, melt-in-the-mouth pedhe from Badayun, brown in colour and decadently rich, with a sprinkling of powdered sugar, and adorned with half a cashew and the famous gazak from Aligarh. The gazak is quintessentially definitive of Aligarh. There is a soft, flaky kind with sesame seeds and a hint of rose. The brittle variety has peanuts in it. We love both kinds and devour them by the box.

Sometimes, we attend the Numaish-special mushaira. There are some other attractions that we pass by rather than stop and engage with. These include the *maut ka kuan*, with bike riders hurtling themselves at breakneck speed along a circular course and performing dangerous stunts; a relic from the olden days, a wooden merry go round known as *charrakh choon*; a circus and a nautanki (a boisterous and lively folk performance). A focal point and also a meeting point for lost children and companions is a fountain, known simply as *Fawwara*. *Baradari*, literally twelve doors, is another important landmark structure. Soon, it is time to head home from this sensory overload of bright and flickering neon lights and the blaring music and announcements. Our bellies are full; we have even polished off the customary softie ice cream. There is nothing else remaining except to gather our precious shopping, do a head count and happily head home.

Needless to say, a trip to the Numaish is absolutely a must during the season, and we have been known to plan a special visit just for the weekend to attend it.

The poet Shakeel Badayuni paints an evocative and lively picture of the atmosphere at the Aligarh Numaish in his poem titled 'Numaish-e-Aligarh'. Here is an excerpt:

Woh pur-kaif aalam woh dilkash nazarey
Woh jalvon ke bahte hue khushk dharey
Woh namkeen aghaz-e-shab Allah Allah
Numaish ki woh tab-o-tab Allah Allah
Woh baab-e-muzammil pe jashn-e-charaaghan
Falak par hon jaise sitaare darakhshaan
Fazaon mein goonje huey woh sitare
Woh jan-bakhsh naġhme woh pur-lutf gaane

(That heady atmosphere, those alluring sights
The razzle and dazzle that flows like a stream
That charming inception of the night, O God
The eagerness and excitement of the Numaish, O God
The stunning display of lights on the Muzammil gate
Like sparkling stars on the night sky
The Tarana echoes through the air
The life-affirming melodies, the joyous songs)

~

Returning to Nanno's home:

The maash ki dal (urad dal) is unlike any other dal we have tasted. It is neither a turmeric-laden yellow one nor a thick liquid in consistency. Each grain of the dal is ivory and separate, and it looks like thousands of miniature pearly baby teeth. It is *khili hui*, as Amma calls it, meaning well-cooked but not mushy. The dal has a precise way of cooking until it just cooks and the grains do not clump together. It is served with a generous garnish of crispy brown, caramelized onion slices and whole dried red chillies fried in ghee. To aid its digestion, ginger juliennes are added to it.

Nanno has invited us all to her house for a daawat, or dinner party. It sounds grand, but it is an informal family affair. We all reach her house on foot, as it is close by. There is a large courtyard with beautiful geometric mosaic and tile patterns on the floor as you enter through the carved wooden gates. There is a chowki similar to Amma's, on which Nanno is sitting, reading a dog-eared copy of *Shama* magazine. She looks delighted to see us all and hugs us warmly. She announces in a mock whisper that her only contribution to the feast has been the maash ki dal, as her daughter-in-law has made chicken qorma. There are rotis, kept warm and soft in a hand-embroidered cotton cloth, and a big *martabaan* (glazed earthenware urn) filled with a water-based pickle, shaljam ka achaar. It has flat chunks of peeled, parboiled turnips steeped in a fiery pickling liquid of red chilli powder, whole cloves of garlic, plenty of salt and mustard seeds, matured gradually over weeks in the gentle winter sunshine. It has a pale orange tint and is sour and piquant in taste. The tiny white specks of mustard, or raii, swirl around in the liquid like a shaken snow globe when the martabaan is held in both hands and given a gentle nudge. The urn is sealed off with a square of muslin cloth, secured with a piece of string. These muslin cloths are washed and reused for years on end until they eventually fall apart and, by this time, have acquired an ecru tint due to exposure to the sun and smears from the pickle. There is a distinct, pungent odour to it, and we scoop a ladleful into a bowl to enjoy it with the meal. This is unlike most pickles, as it is water-based rather than oil-based, but it is unique, very special and seasonal. It elevates the most humble of meals, imparting a burst of flavour, freshness and piquancy. The smell can be a bit overwhelming and strong, but the taste more than makes up for it.

Soon, we are all settled around the large cloth dastarkhwan spread out on her chowki, some of us spilling over to various assorted chairs and *moondey* (wicker stools). The dal is delicious, and we all take second helpings of it. We still have time for *meetha* (dessert), which is gajar ka halwa made with plump and juicy red carrots, khoya (dried whole milk), ghee and sugar. The crumbled, cream-coloured flecks of khoya contrast beautifully with the auburn goodness of the sweet, sumptuous and pleasantly earthy-flavoured halwa. There are slivers of blanched almonds interspersed with the khoya, and it tastes heavenly. It is the perfect ending to a perfect yet simple meal. There is laughter and an air of informality and unforced joviality. All of us have visited the Numaish at some point in the past few days, and we regale one another with our individual experiences. There are animated, though light-hearted, discussions about the food and the wares on display currently. Nanno proudly shows us a beige shawl with a narrow dark brown geometric border that her daughter-in-law brought for her from the Numaish. She is pleased with the colour and softness and the fact that it has no '*phool patti*' (floral embroidery) or *cheekhtey huey rang* (literally colours that shout!). We tell Nanno about our escapades and purchases, and she chuckles when we tell her about the bottles of chuuran.

We understand how the simplest of meals in a convivial, no-fuss environment can be a blessing that soothes the soul, lifts one's spirits and brings people closer. Sharing a meal with loved ones is a special boon, not just a social obligation. We learn this important lesson first-hand through all these relaxed, joyful, at times cacophonous, but never tedious or stressful meals shared with family and extended family. Laughter, along with good food, is certainly the best medicine.

Maash ki Dal

Maash, or urad dal, as it is commonly known, is a staple in most of the homes of our extended family. The way this dal is prepared is different from usual dal dishes, and this method is probably specific to north India, especially Uttar Pradesh. Being 'baadi', or a slightly difficult to digest dal, we prefer to soak it overnight. Some people also add a pinch of asafoetida and/or ginger to it. The dried red chilli in the baghaar gives it a delightfully smoky and intense flavour. This dal might look bland and pale, but it is definitely truly special and sublime.

1 cup urad dal, soaked overnight
1 cup water
salt to taste

For the baghaar:
a bit of ghee or cooking oil
1 small onion, thinly sliced lengthwise
½ tsp cumin seeds
1 whole dried red chilli
fresh ginger juliennes

For the garnish:
chopped green chillies and fresh coriander leaves

Cook the dal along with salt and a few ginger juliennes (save the rest for garnishing) until it is just cooked but not mushy.

Use a heavy-bottomed, open pot to cook rather than a pressure cooker, to avoid overcooking the dal.

Once done, place it in the serving dish and use a fork to gently separate the grains that have clumped together.

In a small pan, heat the ghee or oil, add the cumin seeds, and wait until they splutter. Now add the onion slices and gently fry until they turn brown and crispy.

Add the whole dried red chilli too, and fry until it darkens. Pour this baghaar over the dal.

Garnish the dal further with the desired amount of finely chopped green chillies, a few sprigs of chopped coriander leaves, and a few ginger juliennes scattered on top.

Some people also squeeze a few drops of lemon juice on the dal or serve it with lemon wedges on the side.

Shaljam ka Achar

1 kg turnips
8–10 cloves of garlic
3–4 tbsp red chilli powder
2 tbsp mustard seeds
salt to taste

Wash, peel and chop the turnips into thick slices or discs.

Boil these with water in a large pot.

Place the slices inside a clean and sterilized glass jar, along with the garlic, mustard seeds and chilli powder.

Boil a litre of water, allow it to cool completely, and then pour it over the turnip slices.

Seal it with a cloth and let it sit on a sunny window ledge, or outside if it's sunny.

In a couple of weeks, it will be ready to use with its fiery, tangy, salty goodness.

~

Of course, there are many more family daawats to be had, as all the women in the family are inherently affectionate and great feeders. They take an interest in us gawky teens and include us in their conversations. We are also taught to respect them and their hospitality, eat whatever has been prepared and duly accompany the elders at every daawat we are invited to. We didn't realize it then, but we were honing our own hosting skills and social etiquette in the process. This was a blueprint for our own futures when we grew up and had our own homes. Our accomplishments in our chosen academic fields, our awards, certificates and medals were down to our own hard work, but these important life skills of *khuloos* (affection), *ikhlaq* (affability) and humility were taught to us in these aangans by all these amazing women.

Hum hue tum hue ki 'mir' hue
Us ki zulfon ke sab aseer hue

—Mir Taqi Mir

(You, me or the poet Mir
we are all prisoners of her tresses)

STORIES

Bandariya Bahuriya

(The Monkey Daughter-in-Law)

Long, long ago, there lived a king who had three sons. The princes had reached marriageable ages, and the king and queen were keen to see them married soon.

The royal *najoomi* (astrologer) was sent for. The najoomi stroked his long beard and fell into deep thought. Finally, he spoke:

Jaan ki aman paaoon toh kahoon huzoor (Please pardon my life as I speak, your majesty), one of the sons has a *massla* (problem) with his marriage, but I can't say which one it is. He requested that the princes accompany him to a forest, as he had a *tarkeeb* (solution) in mind.

The king readily agreed.

Once they reached the forest, the najoomi handed each prince a bow and arrow and said, 'In whichever direction your arrow lands, we will send a *rishta* (proposal) for the princess of that land. The eldest son took aim, and the arrow went in the northern direction. The second prince's arrow landed in the southern direction. Then, it was the turn of the youngest prince.

His arrow pierced the tail of a *bandariya* (female monkey) that was sitting on a branch of a tree. And so, while the other brothers wed beautiful and gracious princesses, the poor youngest brother had to wed the bandariya.

Being an obedient and *nek* (noble) son, he brought home his bride but insisted on staying in a smaller palace away from everyone to avoid embarrassment and derision.

One day, the king and queen decided to test the *hunar* (talents) of their new bahus. They were each required to make an embroidered *reshmi rumaal* (silken handkerchief) and present it to the queen.

The princesses promptly got on with the task, each vying to outdo the other in *kasheedakaari* (embroidery) and lacework.

The youngest prince, however, sat forlorn and dejected in his palace. When his monkey bride found out about the test, she said:

'Do not worry, my beloved husband. You get ready to go to the palace.'

As he was leaving, she handed him the most exquisitely beautiful handkerchief to present to the queen.

Next, the king and queen asked their bahus to make biryani to test their cooking prowess. Both princesses spent the day in their royal kitchens, carefully and diligently preparing the most extravagant and superb dish they could. The air was redolent with the aromas of saffron, cardamom, pistachios and almonds fried in *asli* (pure) ghee. The choicest cuts of fresh meat and the most expensive and *naayaab* (rare) mewa-kishmish (dry fruits) were used. Chickens fattened on cashews and raisins, and goats fed on saffron-infused milk were brought to the royal kitchens.

The resultant sumptuous and decadent biryani preparations were duly presented on solid gold platters with precious rubies and emeralds encrusted on the rims, with a great deal of fanfare, and carried in by four uniformed guards.

The king and queen tasted the elder bahu's biryani and then the middle one's. They were both delectable and luxuriously prepared, so they were very impressed.

The youngest prince sat with his head bowed and his brow furrowed. His monkey bride asked him the cause of his sadness. She placed her little hand on his forehead, smoothing the lines and said,

'Do not worry beloved husband, get ready to leave for the palace.'

As he was leaving, she handed him a covered dish to take to the palace.

He placed this dish beside the others in the court. As the gleaming *sarposh* (silver cloche) was lifted, an ambrosial fragrance filled the court. The magnificent aroma reached the surrounding kingdoms as well, and it tasted absolutely divine! Each grain of rice was long, perfect and separate, the meat was flavoursome and succulent and the spices were delicate yet exquisite. The king and queen declared it the winner and said that they had never tasted such a delicious and exquisitely made biryani in their lives. The older bahus were disappointed and sulked in their rooms.

'We now want to see our bahu begums', said the king and queen the next day.

The youngest prince was aghast. Terror gripped his heart in a vice-like grip. Embroidery and cooking were fine but how could

he present his monkey bride in court for all to see? He would
be a laughing stock! He gazed despondently out of the window
and sighed.

His bride asked him the reason for his sadness. When she
came to know, she smiled and asked him to leave for the court,
saying she would follow him in her *palki* (palanquin).

The prince left for the court, and everyone asked him why
his bride had not come. His face reddened, and he looked
embarrassed. The eldest prince's bride looked radiant in her
surkh (red) gharara, laden with *moti-jawahrat* (gemstones). She was
stunning! The middle prince's wife was dressed in a *sabz* (green)
gharara, encrusted with pearls and diamonds. She was beautiful!

Just then, a royal palki stopped at the entrance of the
court. From behind the silken *parda* (curtain), a milky white
foot emerged, wearing a silver *paazeb* (anklet) and a beautiful
mehndi pattern drawn on it. The most breathtakingly beautiful
girl, with long, lustrous black hair that almost reached her feet,
emerald green eyes, skin as smooth as *sang-e-marmar* (marble)
and a delicate build, emerged from the palki and stood beside
the youngest prince. She wore a shimmering white gharara, and
jasmine flowers adorned her hair. Her lips were like delicate
rosebuds, and her long eyelashes fluttered over her milky cheeks.
Her ethereal glow and beauty lit up the entire court, and everyone
else seemed to pale in comparison.

She was the cynosure of all eyes, and everyone was singing
her praises. The prince, mystified and confused, ran to his
palace. On the bed, lay a *chhaal* (monkey hide). Wishing that
the beautiful creature he just saw would remain his forever, the
prince set fire to the skin. As he did so, his beautiful bride felt
a burning sensation in her body and fled in panic. By the time
she found the prince, her skin was badly burnt, and she herself

was in great agony. She collapsed on the floor, writhing in pain. The prince urgently sent for the royal hakim and he tried his potions and *marhams* (balms), but in vain. Hakims and holy men were invited from far-flung places, but no one could help the youngest bride.

Distraught and melancholic, the prince stood under a Champa tree in his garden, contemplating and praying for the life of his wife. He had tears in his eyes. Two birds were sitting on the branches of the tree, and he could hear their conversation.

'How cruel the king of Paristan (the land of fairies) was to punish his only daughter and turn her into a monkey.'

The other bird said:

'Yes, and as if this were not enough, she lies disfigured and in such agony. Little does the prince know that all the hakims in the world will not be able to cure her. However, if he himself makes a paste from the fragrant flowers of this tree and applies it to her skin, she will surely heal.' Then, they flew away.

The prince quickly plucked the flowers and ground them to a paste himself, even though hundreds of servants stood by *haath baandey* (helplessly). He then gently applied the paste to the burns on his wife's skin. As he did so, her injuries disappeared, and she sat up smiling.

Suddenly, a flash of bright light and a sandalwood fragrance filled the room.

It was the king of Paristan, who had come to take his daughter back. She pleaded with her father to let her stay with her husband. The king saw how pure and steadfast the prince's love was, and he let his daughter remain an *insaan* (human). He blessed them both and disappeared.

The *shehzada* (prince) and his beautiful bride lived happily ever after.

The Tale of Haji Baghlol*

Munshi Sajjad Hussain

Note: Haji Baghlol, or rather, his persona, was such a huge part of our lives as children that not only were we told this story, but anyone wearing an oversized, ill-fitting or baggy outfit was immediately dubbed as looking like Haji Baghlol by Amma and to this day, by all of us. So even though my memory of the actual story was sketchy, I had to include it. For the sake of authenticity, I have translated the story from the original Urdu text myself, as accurately as I could. In the present day, some aspects of the story may be considered offensive or insensitive, and I do apologize for that.

Look, Haji Baghlol comes walking by. He is short of stature and has a big paunch. His eyes are sunken, his ears are large and his nose is flat, the nostrils flared. He is as dark as his beard is white.

---

* Translated from the late-nineteenth-century original Urdu text from Rekhta eBooks.

Haji Baghlol wears an achkan that almost reaches his ankles. A big turban is tied around his head. As one of his legs is longer than the other, he limps and often gets entangled in his oversized achkan.

A long time ago, Haji Sahib worked on a ship that transported pilgrims bound for Hajj. He himself had never performed Hajj, but he became known as Haji, a word usually used for one who has done so. Everyone in town knew him well and sometimes teased him. They would make fun of him too, but if Haji Baghlol got annoyed, they would hurriedly placate him.

One must be wary of Haji Baghlol. He is easily angered. In a fit of rage, he can thrash you with his walking stick. He is good at heart, however, and plain-speaking.

Right now, he is deep in thought and mumbling to himself. Let's hear what he says:

'Kya naam ke . . . I must buy a horse! If not a horse, then an animal of some sort—even a donkey—would do. Without a savaari, an animal to ride, life is incomplete. There are many kinds of animals to ride, such as a camel or an elephant, but a donkey is the best. I must go to the auction house to see if I can get myself a nice donkey. It will be great fun!'

Thinking this, Haji Baghlol walked towards his house. On the way, a man asked him:

'Haji Sahib, is all well with you? Where are you rushing off to?'

Haji Baghlol was startled. 'Miya Nazir Husain, it is you! Assalam alaikum!' He excitedly told him his plan to visit an auction house in a garbled, incoherent manner, and asked him to bring along some other friends too. Nazir Hussain politely nodded his head and walked away, quickly making his escape.

It was evening. Haji Baghlol reached home weary and exhausted. He wanted to lie down for some time, but rest was not in his destiny! The thought of travelling to the auction frazzled him, and he immediately set off for the home of Ghissiya, the *tanga* (horse carriage) driver. The poor man was eating his evening meal.

Haji Baghlol said to him,

'We must leave for the auction house at daybreak. We mustn't be late.'

The tanga driver nodded his assent.

Haji Sahib rushed home, threw off his achkan on the bed and turban on a stool, placed his walking stick in a corner, and sat down to eat. But he was distracted; his mind was occupied by the auction house. He gulped down huge mouthfuls of his food and water and lay down in his bed, rubbing his belly.

Very soon, the rooster called out. It was dawn. He hurriedly got up, somehow dressed in odd clothes and picking up his stick, reached Ghissiya's house. The poor man was in deep sleep, dreaming happily. He was startled to see Haji Sahib and hurriedly started getting the tanga ready, cursing him silently. Haji Sahib quickly hopped on to sit on the tanga. The driver held the *lagaam* (reins) in one hand and a *chhabuk* (whip) in the other, and together they set off for the auction house. The tanga's horse was painfully slow and crawled instead of galloping its way to the auction only by late morning. The old and rickety cart of the tanga made a *charrakhhh-choooon* sound during its journey. Once they reached the auction house, Haji Baghlol leapt from the tanga and started looking for his friends in the crowds, wide-eyed.

In his panic, he started calling out each of the people he was expecting to be there by name:

'*Arey bhai* Nazeer Husain, *arey* Maulvi Sahib, Mirza Sahib . . .
Speak up!'

They would have spoken up if any of them were there.

He became despondent and, in his heart, ended his friendship with these men, vowing never to meet them again.

There was a big crowd at the auction house. First, the expensive, well-bred horses were displayed. The cost of these was 200–300 rupees, however, he bid odd amounts of ten or fifteen rupees, needlessly. The people who had come for the auction laughed and jeered at this audacity.

Once the auction of these horses ended, a straggly bunch of tired, old mules remained. Among these, a starved, mangy, worn-out female mule remained. She had a saddle on her back that cleverly concealed her open sores.

Haji Sahib chose her and bid fifteen rupees, looking around proudly.

Just then, a butcher called out a bid of sixteen rupees.

'Nineteen rupees!' thundered Haji Sahib, not to be outdone.

The auctioneer said, 'It's yours for nineteen rupees'.

Haji Sahib eagerly went towards him to pay.

But his hand kept slipping down his side! Looking down, he noticed that in his rush, he had worn his achkan inside out! The group of people standing around him laughed, greatly embarrassing him. He quickly went and changed, then paid the auctioneer.

The assistant auctioneer started taking off the saddle. Haji Baghlol admonished him and rushed towards the animal. He then tried to mount it, waving his stick around in anger. All this commotion scared the poor mule, and she moved away just as Haji Sahib was hopping up to mount.

Haji Sahib fell flat on the ground! The onlookers picked him up, wiped off the dust, and handed him his stick, which had fallen too. Panic soon ensued, and the mule gave an almighty *dulatti* (kick) and trotted away.

An incensed Haji Sahib asked for his money back, but the auctioneer reassured him that his mule would return. And return she did, soon enough.

Haji Sahib approached her gingerly this time. Alas, there was no saddle left on her, as it got thrown off in the melee. He took off his turban, unrolled it and made a sort of lasso with it to walk alongside her.

Back home, he went to buy grains and grass for the mule to eat and also brought home a stable boy to care for her. The stable boy was full of mischief!

He cleaned and saddled up the old mule and called out for Haji Sahib to ride his mule. Soon a crowd gathered to watch, consisting of neighbours and curious passers-by.

Poor Haji Sahib tried a few times to mount, but without success. He got nervous and mistakenly put his right foot in the left stirrup, and so it came to be that he was sitting facing backwards on the poor old mule.

To make matters worse, the stable boy tickled her long, floppy ear and she broke into a sudden canter, with poor Haji Sahib astride, hanging on for dear life. By now, people were calling out and laughing loudly. Suddenly, the poor old mule stumbled and fell along with Haji Sahib too.

After that day, Haji Baghlol said, '*Tauba*', and refused to speak about it, and even avoided any mention of his *ghorhi* (horse).

And if someone were to mention it, he would run after them, stick in hand.

The Fable of Mama Qamas

(The Tale of Mama Qamas)

Long, long ago, there lived one Mama Qamas. She was contemplating marriage with her various suitors. She didn't want to marry someone *aisa-waisa* (ordinary); rather, she thought carefully about each of her prospective grooms with the aim of choosing the best one.

The first to approach her for her hand in marriage was a thief. He promised wealth, albeit ill-gotten, but she reasoned that he would forever be on the run. He was not a stable, reliable man; he could easily abandon her and run away.

What would become of her?

Then there was a peacock, majestic and glorious in his plumage. His preening and beauty captured her attention instantly. He is so handsome to look at. But look at his ugly feet! And he eats nothing but *keedhe-makodhey*—insects, lizards and frogs! How disgusting! That is all we will eat if I marry him. *Tauba!*

What would become of her?

Then there were two brothers, both of whom were keen on marrying her. One came forward and said:

'Marry me, Mama Qamas. I have a wholesale business selling maash ki dal. I have sacks upon sacks of it in my house. You will never go hungry, I promise.'

Pushing him aside, his brother said:

'Me, me, Mama Qamas, marry me. I have a wholesale business selling moong ki dal. I have *hazaron mann* of moong ki dal in my house. You will never go hungry, I promise.'

Mama Qamas thought about this. This is all very well, but that means I can only ever eat either maash ki dal or moong ki dal and nothing else. What if I get tired of eating only one kind of dal?

What would become of me?

Her final suitor was a rat, Mooshaji. 'I will treat you like a queen and shower you with my love. I can go anywhere and get you the most exquisite and naayab fabrics, like *athlas*, *kamkhab* and *asharfi poth* to wear. Laddoo, perhey, imarti, pistey-badaam to eat, and *heerey-moti* to adorn yourself with. You will want for nothing, my *jaan-e-bahaar*, my *dilruba*.'

Mama Qamas was delighted to hear all this. This seemed ideal, and Mooshaji was an ardent and affectionate suitor. Her life would be like heaven on earth.

She accepted his *rishta* (proposal). There was a wedding with *dhoom-dhaam* (celebratory pomp and show). Mooshaji brought his newly-wed bride home. True to his word, he would sneak into *kothris* (storerooms) where expensive brocades and silks were stored. He would steal them and proudly present them to his wife. He would hover near weddings and *daawats* (feasts) and steal the choicest of foods: mithai made with asli ghee, fluffy sheermal, delectable tandoori murgh morsels, and all kinds of delicious and rich foods. He would steal *gehne-zewar* (jewellery), a *haar* (necklace) here, a ring there, and a pair of *jhumke karanphool* (earrings) there.

Mama Qamas led a blissful life, surrounded by luxury and riches. Her slightest wish was Mooshaji's command. She had the most gorgeous, shimmering outfits to wear and lounged around all day, nibbling pistey-badaam. Her *razai* (quilt) was made of *makhmal* (velvelt) and pure gold *zari*, and her shawl was the softest pashmina. She lived like a queen and was very happy with her life.

Now, the people living in the area were fed up with the menace of rats pilfering their food and valuables and damaging their clothes. One night, they decided to set a trap.

Khatttt! went the trap, with Mooshaji inside it. Try as he might, he could not free himself and was killed by the people who had set the trap, and he was thrown away with the rubbish.

Mama Qamas was devastated when she found out.

She wailed:

'*Moong waley chhorhey, Maash waley chhorey*
Chhorha nachta mor
Mama bechari kya karey
Mooshaji nikley chor'

(I rejected moong sellers, and maash sellers
I rejected a dancing peacock
O what can I do?
My Mooshaji turned out to be a thief)

The Legend of Noble Naseem and Cunning Husnara

Naseem lived with her stepmother, Hafiza Bi, and stepsister, Husnara, in a small house in a village. Her father, who loved her dearly, had died a few years ago, and the family was poor. Naseem helped with cooking, cleaning and helping her stepmother with her itr or perfume-making business. Hafiza Bi would collect naayab and fragrant flowers and mix them with herbs and *nakhh*, a resin, to make precious itr that she sold in coloured glass bottles. It was difficult and time-consuming, and she earned just enough to get by. Husnara sat on a *takht* (seat) all day, preening herself and making patterns on her hands and feet with the juice of flowers.

One day, Hafiza required some flowers that grew in the forest and asked Naseem to go and pick them for her. Naseem dutifully set off with a wicker basket and walked for several *kos* (miles) to reach the tree her mother had told her about. She noticed that the tree grew in the private front garden of a dilapidated, small cottage. Naseem politely knocked on the door and entered, as it was open. An old lady with wild, unkempt hair and dirty clothes lay on a *khaat* (cot) made of *sutli* (twine). Her tattered, old razai had fallen on the floor, and she seemed too weak to pick it up. Naseem felt sad at the sorry state of the poor old woman and placed her razai back on the bed after shaking it free of dust. She then combed and braided the woman's hair. She wiped her face with a damp cloth and made a quick hot meal of khichdi, as it looked like the woman had not eaten for days. She then cleaned the cottage and sat down beside her. She asked if she could pluck some flowers from the tree outside.

The old lady nodded, so Naseem bade her farewell and went outside. The flowers had an intense, intoxicating and unique fragrance. She plucked some and happily made her way home. Her stepmother would be pleased, she thought.

However, when she reached home, her stepmother angrily shouted:

'Where have you been all day? We have been waiting. We have no food, and the house is an untidy mess. The clothes are unwashed and the dishes are dirty.'

Naseem saw Husnara lounging lazily on the takht, sulking and pouting.

As she opened her mouth to explain, pearls sprung out and bounced off her tongue. They fell to the floor, and the stepmother was shocked. She picked one up gingerly and held it against the light. A pure Basra pearl, *beshqeemti* (precious) and beautiful. A small heap of them lay on the floor. Hafiza Bi rushed and got a *reshmi rumal* (silk handkerchief) to gather them up in.

'What have you been up to, you wretched girl? Where did you steal these pearls?

She asked, giving her a resounding slap.

Poor Naseem, shocked and terrified as she was with the pearls flowing from her mouth, started to cry.

Lo and behold!

Each tear drop as it travelled down from the corner of her beautiful, almond-shaped eye, down her *marmareen* (alabaster), petal-soft cheek, became a tiny but perfectly formed diamond.

Hafiza Bi was speechless. She carefully picked up the gems and placed them in her *batua* (purse). She sat down on the takht, in shock and disbelief, and demanded Naseem tell her everything. Naseem did so.

Hafiza Bi decided that her own daughter too should go to this magical tree. She was already thinking about the gems and riches she could amass if these were to double. She would live in a mansion, waited upon by maids and servants, who would fan her and press her feet. She would wear athlas, kamkhab and the finest silks, a *rani haar* made of pure gold, eat murgh mutanjan every day and bathe in perfumes . . . It would be a glorious life!

As she laughed and danced around the tiny room, her daughters began to laugh, too. The only difference was that when Naseem laughed, flowers sprayed forth from her mouth. They fell at her feet, fresh and fragrant: jasmine, roses and champa.

'No time to waste', Hafiza Bi wailed. 'Go now', she said, pushing Husnara out through the door.

Husnara sullenly walked the distance until she came to the tree and stretched her hand to pluck a flower. However, whenever she tried to reach a flower, it seemed to move away from her. She stood on her toes and muttered irritably. She thought of getting a *moonda*, or footstool, of some sort from the cottage nearby. She barged in and started to *khakorh* (rummage) around. She heard an old woman cry out for water, but she ignored her.

'Stay silent, you old hag! I am looking for a stool', Husnara barked.

She haughtily carried the stool out, but now, all the flowers had shed and lay on the ground, looking bruised and brown in colour. She grabbed them, stuffed them in her basket and hurried home before it was dark.

When she reached home, her mother expectantly opened the door. Alas, her *laadli*, her precious child, had horns growing on either side of her head, like a goat, arching and pointy. She was horrified!

Looking at her mother's horror-stricken face, she asked, 'What happened, Ammi?'

As the words came out of her mouth, so did several live frogs.

Trrr trrr trrr

They hopped around her feet, filling the room with a sickening stench like a *keechadh bhari nali* (dirty drain).

The mother and daughter clung to one another, and Husnara suddenly caught a glimpse of herself in a mirror on the wall.

Hai! she exclaimed, and she started to cry. Each tear turned into a live lizard, slithering down her neck and back and licking her arms with its slimy tongue.

It tickled her arms, and she started to laugh uncontrollably.

And as Husnara laughed, head lice shot out of her mouth, biting her on the face and neck. They crawled and made patterns on her skin, with bites and blood, in circles, lines and the *phool-bootey* designs she loved to adorn her skin . . .

She ran out screaming and was never seen again.

Raja Bakarkana, the Goat-Eared King

Once upon a time, there was a king. He lived in a magnificent palace and had wealth, horses, elephants and huge areas of land. However, he had a shameful secret too. His ears were like those of a goat—large, floppy and cascading from the top of his royal head with a conical, hairy end as big as each of his hands. When he was born, he had a pair of pointy, upturned ears, and as he grew older, his ears too grew. The king was very embarrassed by this and wore his hair in long tresses, his *taj*, or crown, majestically poised to hide the deformity. For this reason, he would never get his hair cut, and let it grow.

When his hair became so long that it reached the ground, it was decided to summon the kingdom's top barber. The king took him aside and swore him to secrecy. The barber agreed, and in the confines of the king's personal chamber, he began to ply his trade. The locks of hair fell to the ground, and there was an audible gasp from the barber. The king reminded him of his promise of silence and sent the barber away.

The barber went home, and his wife excitedly asked him about his royal encounter. Bound by secrecy, the barber said nothing. The next day, his friends asked him about his visit to the royal court, and he brushed it off again. The day after, his customers tried to get some royal gossip from him too. But he remained quiet, as he had promised the king.

But by now, the barber could bear it no longer. His stomach ached with the burden of the secret. He just could not keep it to himself anymore.

Clutching his stomach, he ran to the forest. He looked around; there was not a single person to be seen. A deer stood among the trees, alone and old. Who can he tell, the barber wondered? So he whispered in the ear of the deer about his secret and immediately felt relieved.

Then he happily went home and carried on with his life.

Meanwhile, a hunter passed through the same forest and killed the deer. He took the meat home to cook and left the skin behind. When he ate the deer meat, he began to shout at the top of his voice:

'*Raja bakarrrr kanaa, Raja bakarrrr kana.*'

News of this reached the king, and he was furious. He ordered the beheading of the hunter as well as the barber. His secret was safe now, and no one else would know, he thought to himself, relieved.

A passing musical troupe stopped to rest in the forest. They were going to play at the royal court.

One of the tabla drums had got damaged and its *jhilli*, or skin, needed to be changed.

The deer skin lying on the grass was cleaned and stretched carefully across the drum.

They had some food and drank water from the cool stream nearby. Feeling rested, they made their way to the royal court.

They were welcomed with great fanfare and jubilation. The singers seated themselves on expensive Persian carpets, and their accompanying musicians sat alongside. The court was packed with people wishing to listen to the famous singer, who enthralled all with her *thumris* and ghazals. Courtiers in their finery, distinguished writers, poets, officials and other important people were all there. The singers were getting started, and to accompany them, the *tabalchi* (tabla player) began to play. Loud and clear, a sound came from the tabla:

Raja bakarrrrrkana, Raja bakarrrrrrkana . . .

The Tale of Sharif Khan and Badmash Khan

Once there were two brothers who lived with their parents in a small hut in a village. One day, as their mother was cooking, a stray *chingari* (spark) touched the hut made of twigs, pieces of wood and straw. It burned down, and both parents died. The brothers, named Sharif Khan and Badmash Khan, were left orphaned and penniless. They decided to set out into the world to find a livelihood. After walking for two days in the dense jungle and surviving on wild berries and water from streams, they reached a huge mansion. There were orchards of luscious fruit and fields of vegetables and grains surrounding it that stretched for miles, as far as the eye could see. Badmash Khan said to his brother, 'Why don't you try and see if you can get some work and then we can eat'. Sharif, the younger brother, nodded and set off.

He walked to an old bargad tree, where he saw some people sitting under its shade. Panna Seth sat there, twirling his well-oiled moustache, surrounded by a few servants. He sat on a red *makhmal gaddi* (velvet cushion) and wore several necklaces of gold and rubies. He sat there puffing at his hookah, which made gurgling noises, the rings on his fat, hairy fingers glinting in the sun. The other men hovered respectfully or sat *ukkrhoon* (on their haunches) around him on the ground. One pressed his feet, another fanned him with a big hand-held *pankha*, or fan, and yet another sat bent over a ledger, writing assiduously in it. Sharif approached Panna Seth timidly and asked with folded hands if he could get some work.

Panna Seth looked at his dishevelled state and said, 'You see all these fields and orchards. The crop is ripe, and the harvest needs to be done. If you can do it, at the end of the day, you bring a leaf, and you will be given enough food to cover the leaf. You will be paid afterwards. *Manzoor hai* (Do you agree)?'

Sharif nodded and set off, working tirelessly in the fields as the burning sun scorched his back, and thirst and hunger gnawed at his stomach. He picked dozens of ripe, juicy mangoes, fragrant and luscious melons, shiny purple brinjals, plump and speckled kaddu and turai, that looked like coarse-skinned fingers of an angry green deo, and big and bulbous lauki that looked like a *tamancha*, or baton, to fight off any attackers. By evening, he had filled 106 boxes. He was to get an anna for each box and was looking forward greatly to the meal and payment. He wondered if there would be hot rotis and dal, and maybe some alu (potatoes) too. Perhaps there would be kheer afterwards, since the *seth* (boss) looked so wealthy and lived in a huge mansion. He licked his cracked and dried lips in anticipation.

However, as he was completely exhausted, he could only pluck a leaf from the imli (tamarind) tree close by. He slowly trudged to the kitchen, where he was given just enough food to cover the imli leaf and water to drink.

Hungry and tired, he went to Panna Seth for his money. Panna Seth said, 'I have one condition before I pay you. If you can put fire inside a paper without burning it, you can have the money.' Sharif scratched his head and tried in vain several times to fulfil this task. Each time he took the *diya salai*, or matchstick, to the scraps of paper, they burned instantly. It was impossible! The ash and scorched bits of paper, strewn around him, mocked him just as Panna Seth and his posse did. Eventually, he gave up and went to sleep, hungry and exhausted on the uneven ground, with sharp pebbles digging into his body and insects crawling all over him and biting him.

The next morning, his brother came to him, and Sharif recounted his ordeal. Badmash had been inspecting the orchards and the area surrounding them the previous day. He had also helped himself to a few juicy guavas from the low-hanging branches near the boundary and drunk cool water from the well. In the evening, he went to the langar at the nearby masjid and ate a hearty meal of pulao and zarda. As a *musafir*, or traveller, he was given shelter for the night and slept soundly. It was now time for him to go to work.

He too approached Panna Seth with joined palms and said he was poor and hungry. Panna Seth was thrilled. Two idiots, desperate but strong, one after the other! *Ahmaqon ki kami nahi!* He rubbed his hands together with glee and repeated the same instructions to Badmash. Badmash, who had identified himself as Baddu to quell any mistrust arising from his name, pretended that he was hearing all this for the first time and thanked him profusely. He then went to the far end of the fields and had a leisurely nap among the gently swaying sugarcane, making a pillow with some of the soft inner leaves. When it was time to eat, he plucked the largest, greenest banana leaf from the clump of fruit trees at the far end and carried it straight to the kitchen. The poor cook ladled large quantities of food on it, and Badmash had a leisurely, filling meal. He wolfed down the rice, dal and gobhi ki sabzi. On his way out, he quietly picked up a laddoo from a pile on the *tashtari* (salver) that was meant for Panna Seth. It was made with asli ghee and studded with pistey-badaam. He bit into it, and the aroma of the ghee and cardamom and the exquisite sweetness of the laddoo, bursting with mewa, pleased him greatly. He picked up a few more and wrapped them in his *rumal* (handkerchief). He carefully arranged the remaining laddoos by hiding a clump of *ghas-phhoos*, or hay, under them. It looked like a perfect pile of laddoos, ready for the greedy and fat mouth of Panna Seth.

Then he quietly picked up all the boxes from the *kothri*, or storage area, that his brother had filled the previous day and stood near them, pretending to look tired and sweaty, facing Panna Seth. He wiped his forehead and sighed dramatically.

Panna Seth posed the same question to him. Badmash thought for a minute and then held aloft a Diwali *qandeel*, a paper lantern, with a lit candle inside it. Fire inside the paper! The coloured strips of shiny paper that hung from it rustled and twinkled, and the flame burned steadily within, shining through the coloured paper patterns in the qandeel.

Panna Seth was astounded!

However, he had no choice but to pay up. Badmash made a hasty departure, lest his crookedness be revealed, and took his brother with him. He shared the money and laddoos with him, and they decided to go elsewhere to work.

The Lioness and the Ewe

A lioness and an ewe were very good friends, or *jigri dost*.

They roamed the jungle together and chatted happily with one another.

They sat by the bank of a river, among the wildflowers, butterflies and songbirds, for hours on end.

They confided in one another, offering sincere advice and words of solace where needed. *Dukh sukh ke sathi.*

The lioness soon became a mother to a playful, silky-coated cub. Around the same time, the ewe also gave birth to a little lamb, milky white and furry. The days passed happily, the two offspring playing together, chasing one another through the tall grasslands, laughing and having fun. *Mauj ke din.* The lioness and the ewe lay on the grass, smiling indulgently and sighing contentedly.

The names of the little ones, you ask?

The cub was named Sheru.

And the lamb was named Qulmuliya.

With the abundance of juicy fruit, fresh, plump grass, clean drinking water and fresh air, both thrived and were very healthy and well fed. They both had fat cheeks, chubby legs and well-rounded tummies. *Gol matol.* Their eyes sparkled, and their coats shone brightly in the sunlight.

One day, the lioness lay sprawled on the velvety grass on the riverside, idly contemplating her wonderful life, when she had a sudden thought. Her smile widened, and she closed her eyes to fully experience the joyful prospect.

How delicious would little Qulmuliya be, she wondered? Just look at those juicy thighs, his chubby neck with rolls of gently rolling fat, and oh, just look at those cushiony, ample flanks, simply begging to be ripped apart with sharp teeth and savoured . . .

No, I cannot think like that. My dear friend's child. She tried to push the thought out of her mind, but try as she might, she could not stop thinking about it.

An opportunity presented itself the very next day. The ewe had to go away to attend a wedding and asked her friend to look after Qulmuliya.

The lioness agreed readily, almost smacking her lips in anticipation. *Wah wah!*

She hatched a cunning plan and laid their beds side by side for the friends to sleep in once they had finished playing. She would bide her time till night fell and the little ones were fast asleep.

However, Qulmuliya was very clever and sensed the lioness's intentions. As darkness fell, he quietly crept out of his bed and gently rolled the sleeping cub onto his own bed. He quietly slipped away, hiding in the dark shadows just outside the house.

Later that night, the lioness quietly crept over, murmuring softly:

Qulmuliya beta naram naram
Qulmuliya beta garam garam,
Qulmuliya badey maze ka

(Son Qulmuliya, so soft
Son Qulmuliya, so warm
Qulmuliya, so delicious)

With that, she dug her sharp teeth into a juicy neck, savouring a rounded belly and munching on a succulent, tender thigh, mmmm . . .

Just then, a lifeless paw brushed her cheek. In the darkness, she fumbled and pushed it out of her way. It was then that she noticed claws on the paws and cried out!

Hai!

She realized her terrible mistake and screamed, rushing out in blind panic.

She ran out in the darkness, her wails echoing straight into the depths of the deep, inky river outside, and was never seen again.

Ghayab gulla.

As for Qulmuliya, he happily lived with his mother in the jungle. *Hashshass bashshash.*

Khatam shud!

The Ghost Who Lisped

A young woman lived alone in a cottage at the edge of town. Her husband had gone to a place far, far away for work. She spent her time cooking, cleaning and tending to her goat and chickens.

One day a *bhoot* (ghost) happened to pass by her home. He was mischievous and decided to pester this naïve and credulous woman. He assumed the shape and form of an ordinary human and approached her house.

'I have a message from your husband,' he announced.

The woman eagerly opened the door to let him in. He rode a horse and wore a *surkh*, red silk kurta pyjama with a matching embroidered waistcoat. On his head was a jet-black turban, edged with *sunehri gota* (gold ribbon). In his pocket was a matching zariwala rumal. He looked important.

He dismounted and entered the house. As he did so, the woman noticed he had a strange speech impediment, a nasal tone of voice.

And soon, she realized with great horror that he was a bhoot.

How? She had found human bones and vials of blood in his bag.

And he was here to stay!

'*Aaj se ye ghan mena!*'

('This house is mine from now')

From that day on her life was a misery. He killed her goat and chickens, ripping their throats. He also killed many children, men and women in the neighbourhood. He made her cook his favourite meals and oil his hair with *chameli ka tel* (jasmine oil). She lived in fear and was forbidden from ever venturing out.

One day as he lay sleeping, she quietly went to his room, wore his clothes and went out, riding on his horse.

She had left a karahi full of hot oil on the fire and with the help of a string, tied a dripping wet rag high over the karahi.

Every now and then a drop of water would fall in the karahi.

chunnnn chhhunnn chunnnn

The sizzling sound made the ghost think that the woman was cooking. Maybe she is frying pooris, he thought, licking his lips. He would eat them with asli ghee laden suji ka halwa. Mmmm.

He looked out of the window in his room and saw a figure in the distance, dressed just like him.

'*Mema hi sa ghona, mena hi sa jona*
ye kaun hai?'

('An outfit like mine, a horse like mine,

Who is it?')

There was no reply.

As the figure approached, he repeated: *Mena sa jona, mena hi sa ghona*

Ye kaun hai?

Very soon, he saw the horse outside the house sans rider. He turned around, but the woman was too quick. She captured him in a large sack and held the opening tight in her clenched fist.

'*Nikano mujhe, nikano mujhe* (Let me out, let me out)' he pleaded.

There you go, said she, emptying the contents of the sack in the cauldron of boiling, bubbling oil.

The bhoot was never seen again and the woman lived happily ever after.

Kahani khatam, paisa hazam.

The story ends, the money is gone.

Acknowledgements

This book came into being over thousands of animated discussions on video chats in the past years. My mother, Mahjabeen Jalil, deserves the biggest thanks for her patience and excellent recall. I am greatly indebted to my sisters, Rakhshanda and Zarine, for their endless support and encouragement.

I am eternally grateful to Ranjana Sengupta at A Suitable Agency for her unfaltering belief and help.

I am also very thankful to Chirag Thakkar, Commissioning Editor at Penguin Random House India, for his impeccable eye for detail and for his tireless work in getting this book off the ground.

I am indebted to Penguin Random House India for considering and giving a lot of love to my rather quirky memoir.

I would like to thank a very special person, Prof. Pasha M. Khan, Chair in Urdu Language at McGill University, Montreal, who, through his online classes in Urdu poetry appreciation, rekindled my passion for Urdu poetry.

A huge thanks to my daughters, Alvira and Fiza, and to my husband, Khalid, for reading my manuscript and offering very important feedback. Thanks for the unconditional love and absolute trust.

Acknowledgements

This book came into being over thousands of animated discussions and voice chats in the past years. My mother, Mahjabeen Jaffri, deserves the biggest thanks for her patience and excellent recall. I am greatly indebted to my sisters, Raunshanda and Zaima, for their endless support and encouragement.

I am eternally grateful to Kanishka Gupta at AS Literary Agency for her unflinching belief and help.

I am also very thankful to Chiraj Thakkar, Commissioning Editor at Penguin Random House India, for his appreciative eye for detail and for his perseverance in getting this book off the ground.

I am indebted to Penguin Random House India, for considering and giving a lot of love to my rather quirky memoir.

I would like to thank a very special person, Prof. Pasha M. Khan, Chair in Urdu Language at McGill University, Montreal, who, through his online classes in Urdu poetry appreciation, rekindled my passion for Urdu poetry.

A huge thanks to my daughters, Alvira and Fiza, and to my husband, Khalid, for reading my manuscript and offering very important feedback. Thanks for the unconditional love and absolute trust.

Scan QR code to access the
Penguin Random House India website